SOCIALISM AND D

Also by David McLellan

ENGELS
KARL MARX: Early Texts
*KARL MARX: His Life and Thought
KARL MARX: Selected Writings
KARL MARX: The Legacy
MARX
*KARL MARX: Interviews and Recollections (*editor*)
MARX: The First 100 Years
IDEOLOGY
*MARXISM AFTER MARX
*MARX BEFORE MARXISM
*MARX'S *GRUNDRISSE*
*THE THOUGHT OF KARL MARX
*THE YOUNG HEGELIANS AND KARL MARX
*MARXISM AND RELIGION
*SOCIALISM AND MORALITY (*editor with Sean Sayers*)
*SIMONE WEIL: Utopian Pessimist

Also by Sean Sayers

HEGEL, MARX AND DIALECTIC: A Debate (*with Richard Norman*)
REALITY AND REASON
*SOCIALISM AND MORALITY (*editor with David McLellan*)

**Also published by Macmillan*

Socialism and Democracy

Edited by

David McLellan
Professor of Political Theory
University of Kent at Canterbury

and

Sean Sayers
Senior Lecturer in Philosophy
University of Kent at Canterbury

MACMILLAN

First published 1991

Published by
MACMILLAN ACADEMIC AND PROFESSIONAL LTD
Houndmills, Basingstoke, Hampshire RG21 2XS
and London
Companies and representatives
throughout the world

Filmset by Wearside Tradespools, Fulwell, Sunderland

Printed in Hong Kong

British Library Cataloguing in Publication Data
Socialism and democracy.
1. Socialism. Implications of democracy
I. McLellan, David *1940–* II. Sayers, Sean
335
ISBN 0–333–53555–3 (hardcover)
ISBN 0–333–53556–1 (paperback)

Contents

Preface

The following papers were all presented at the joint philosophy/politics graduate seminar (Lentils seminar) held weekly in David McLellan's house during the academic year 1989–90. The quality of these seminars has owed much to the lively contributions of students and staff. This seminar has been running for a number of years and has been able to invite outside speakers through the generosity of the Faculties of Humanities and of Social Sciences in the University of Kent.

DAVID MCLELLAN
SEAN SAYERS

Notes on the Contributors

Gregory Claeys is Associate Professor of History at Washington University, St Louis. He is the author of *Machinery, Money and the Millennium: From Moral Economy to Socialism, 1815–1860*, *Citizens and Saints: Politics and Anti-Politics in Early British Socialism* and *Thomas Paine: Social and Political Thought*.

Peter Ferdinand was Lecturer in Politics at Warwick University from 1976 to 1989; since October 1989 he has been Head of the Asia Pacific Programme, Royal Institute of International Affairs, London. He is the author of various works on the comparative politics of communist regimes, focusing particularly on the USSR, China and Yugoslavia.

Andrew Gamble is Professor of Politics at the University of Sheffield. His publications include *Britain in Decline* and *The Free Economy and the Strong State*. He is currently working on a book on Hayek.

John Hoffman is a Senior Lecturer in Politics at the University of Leicester. His books include *Marxism and the Theory of Praxis*, *The Gramscian Challenge* and *State, Power and Democracy*. His most recently published work, *Building Tomorrow Today*, deals with the development of cooperatives in his native Zimbabwe.

John Keane is Professor of Politics at the Polytechnic of Central London and Director of the Centre for the Study of Democracy in London. Among his books are *Public Life and Late Capitalism* and *Democracy and Civil Society*. He is completing a political biography of Tom Paine.

David McLellan is Professor of Political Theory at the University of Kent. He has recently published *Simone Weil: Utopian Pessimist* (1989) and is working on the political implications of religious belief.

Michael Rustin is Professor of Sociology at the Polytechnic of East London. He is the author of *For a Pluralist Socialism* and many articles on political topics. He is a member of the Council of Charter 88.

Richard Sakwa is Lecturer in the Government and Politics of the USSR at the University of Kent at Canterbury. He is the author of *Soviet Communists in Power: A Study of Moscow during the Civil War, 1918–21* and *Soviet Politics: An Introduction*. He is currently working on a general analysis of perestroika called *Gorbachev and his Reforms* and is also preparing a monograph on the state, democracy and civil society in the USSR, together with an analysis of the New Economic Policy in Moscow, 1921–5.

Anne Showstack Sassoon is Reader in Politics, Kingston Polytechnic. She studied in the US, Italy, and Britain. Her interest in the Nordic countries goes back to the time she was an exchange student in Finland. She is author of *Gramsci's Politics* and editor of *Approaches to Gramsci* and *Women and the State*.

Sean Sayers teaches philosophy at the University of Kent at Canterbury. He was one of the founding editors of *Radical Philosophy*. With Peter Osborne he has edited *Socialism, Feminism and Philosophy: A Radical Philosophy Reader*, and, with David McLellan, *Socialism and Morality*. His publications include (with Richard Norman) *Hegel, Marx and Dialectic: A Debate* and *Reality and Reason: Dialectic and the Theory of Knowledge*. He is currently writing a book on work and human nature.

Hilary Wainwright is at present Senior Simon Research Fellow at the Department of Sociology, Manchester University. Her books include *Labour: A Tale of Two Parties*, (with Sheila Rowbotham and Lynne Segal) *Beyond the Fragments*, and (with Dave Elliot) *The Lucas Plan: A New Trade Unionism in the Making*. She is at present working on a book about new forms of democracy in Europe. She is a member of the Socialist Society.

Fred Whitemore is a Lecturer in Politics and Government at the University of Kent. He has taught and researched in the area of British labour history, socialist thought and British local government. He is also leader of the Labour Group on the Canterbury City Council.

1 Introduction

Sean Sayers

The relationship between socialism and democracy is at the very centre of current political debate. It has been placed there most dramatically by the changes which have been sweeping through the communist world; but related issues are also raised by the new political forces and movements which have been emerging in the West. For the left, particularly, these developments necessitate a profound questioning and rethinking of attitudes to democracy. This is the purpose of the present volume.

Throughout the last century and during the early years of this one, the struggle for democracy was focused primarily on the winning of basic liberal democratic reforms: on extending the franchise and ensuring basic civil rights. Increasingly, indeed, democracy has come to be understood by many people almost exclusively in these liberal terms. Thus democracy is standardly equated with a pluralistic and representative political system, based on universal and equal adult suffrage, together with a structure of 'democratic' rights – freedom of speech, freedom of political association and the 'rule of law' – necessary to ensure that the system does function effectively as a pluralistic one. This is true not only in the West, where liberal democracies in this sense are the established norm, but also in the communist world and elsewhere, where movements for reform often have this system as their goal.

The left's attitude to liberal democracy has been complex and ambivalent. On the one hand, historically socialists played a leading role in the long struggle for liberal reforms: for extensions of the franchise, and for democratic rights and freedoms. These reforms were initially opposed not only by conservatives, but by all but the most radical of liberals as well, who feared that democracy would mean rule by the ignorant and envious multitude, and that it would result in the destruction of property and the civilized order. It is particularly worth recalling this at present, when it is regularly argued by conservatives that socialism and democracy are incompatible. On the other hand, socialists and radicals have also traditionally criticized the liberal conception of democracy as narrow, limited, insufficient and unsatisfactory. Two strands of criticism may be distinguished, although in practice they often overlap and merge. Both arise from the view – which is central to the socialist conception – that genuine democracy must involve popular power.

In the first place, representative democracy is often criticized as a minimal and inadequate form. The idea of democracy is that people should directly and actively participate in the decisions which affect their lives. In a representative system, by contrast, the people as a whole are specifically excluded from direct decision making, which is made the task of a small elected group. Running through the socialist tradition has therefore been the search for fuller and more direct forms of democracy. These ideas are often rejected as impractical and utopian in the context of a modern industrial society. Nevertheless they have had a continuing influence on the left. In recent years, indeed, there has been a marked revival of interest in them, both in the West and in the East; and this is evident in a number of pieces in this collection (for example, Rustin, Wainwright, Sakwa).

The second strand of criticism focuses on the narrowness of the liberal conception of democracy, and is associated particularly with Marxism. The liberal notion conceives of democracy in formal and procedural terms; it makes democracy into a purely political and legal matter. For Marx, however, the real basis of power lies in the class character of society, in its economic and social structure. The enormous differences in wealth and privilege which are characteristic of capitalist society are differences of effective power. Established interests can use the political and legal systems to their own ends; while to the poor and underprivileged, the right to vote and to legal redress often means nothing. Socialists have thus insisted that genuine democracy must go beyond political and legal arrangements, and tackle also the economic and social roots of class inequalities.

Both these strands of thought lead towards the idea of a truer and fuller, socialist form of democracy, distinct from the liberal representative form. However there has been a good deal of ambiguity about the relation between these two forms of democracy, particularly in the Marxist tradition. At times, Marx and other Marxists regard the socialist form of democracy as the extension and completion of the process of democratization initiated with the introduction of liberal democracy, in which its rights and freedoms are preserved and extended. At other times, however, socialist democracy is pictured as an alternative to liberal democracy, which will supersede and replace it.

The latter view was the one that prevailed in the Soviet Union and the other actually existing socialist societies which were modelled on it. These regimes rejected liberal democracy, and claimed instead to be 'People's Democracies', which was supposed to be an alternative and superior form. Since the 1930s, these claims have lacked all credibility. They have now been totally swept away with the collapse of these regimes throughout Eastern Europe.

According to the right, this is proof positive that socialism and democracy are incompatible, and a refutation of the socialist idea of democracy. Such triumphalism is perhaps to be expected; nevertheless, it is premature. There is nothing in recent events, dramatic as they have been, to justify these conclusions – that, at least, is the view taken by all the contributors to this volume. On the other hand, there is also agreement that socialist ideas about democracy now require the most fundamental and radical reassessment. In particular, there is an urgent need to distinguish what remains valid and relevant in the tradition of socialist criticism of liberal democracy, from what is discredited and refuted.

Moreover, there is agreement that the left must now unambiguously acknowledge the value and importance of the achievements of liberal democracy. Pluralistic political institutions and democratic rights form necessary elements for a democratic society in the modern world. This is perhaps the main lesson to be drawn from the collapse of communist power in Eastern Europe.

It is beyond that point that the present debate really begins. Can liberal democracy now be regarded as a sufficient aim for socialists? How much of the traditional critique of liberal democracy remains valid in the modern world? Do direct and participatory forms of democracy have any place in modern society? Should socialists now abandon the idea of a distinctively socialist form of democracy, and confine themselves to furthering and completing the project of liberal democracy?

The first group of papers take up these issues in broad theoretical terms. John Keane (Chapter 2) presents the fundamental issue here in clear and provocative terms. He argues strongly that the left must now abandon the idea of an alternative, socialist form of democracy, whether based on the idea of the removal of class differences, or on direct popular participation. It must overcome its ambivalence, and define itself in terms of its commitment to democracy, conceived along classic liberal lines as involving a pluralistic and representative political system and guaranteed civil rights. Similar ideas are also the subject of Andrew Gamble's contribution (Chapter 3). He begins with a clear and useful review of some influential recent work on the non-Marxist left which, like Keane, argues that the completion of the project of liberal democracy is now not only a necessary but also the sufficient task of socialism. However, he concludes by expressing a series of doubts about these ideas, and affirming the continuing validity of the traditional socialist criticisms of liberal democracy. John Hoffman (Chapter 4) also focuses on the issue between liberal and socialist ideas of democracy, but in a quite different way. Liberalism is a product of capitalism, he argues. However the logic of liberalism, like that of capitalism, is self-transcending; it will ultimately propel society beyond the limits of the liberal democratic state and, indeed, of the state as such. Only then, with the abolition of the state, will true democracy be possible.

The changes in the communist world have been so dramatic and far reaching that they have tended to dominate recent discussion of democracy on the left. However developments in the advanced capitalist world have also had an important influence on the current debate. In particular the experience of the new political movements, like the women's and environmental movements, has initiated new thinking about the strengths and limitations of liberal democracy and the alternatives to it. The next group of papers draws on this experience to explore these questions. Michael Rustin (Chapter 5) begins with a consideration of the democratic reform programme of the Charter 88 movement in Britain. He criticizes it for its characteristically liberal focus on constitutional and political issues. On that basis he explores ways in which ordinary citizens may be enabled to gain more control and participation in some crucial areas of modern life. Hilary Wainwright (Chapter 6) draws on a variety of recent initiatives and experiments in Europe, both East and West, to argue that new forms of democratic participation, administration and regulation are required if disempowered groups are to be drawn into the political process, and their concerns and needs catered for. At a more theoretical level, Anne Sassoon (Chapter 7) discusses the limitations of liberal individualism in the light of the experience of the women's movement. She argues that the problems of ensuring the participation of women and other disadvantaged groups may require a questioning of some of the most basic assumptions of the liberal tradition – assumptions which have been shared by many socialists.

The papers in the final group survey some of the historical and contemporary developments, both in Britain and the communist world, which form the context for these ideas and controversies. Gregory Claeys (Chapter 8) provides a broad and illuminating overview of the ideas of the Owenite socialists in the first half of the last century. He criticizes Marx and Engels' dismissive description of these early socialists as mere 'utopians'. He shows how they anticipated many of the controversies which are still current on the left (and exemplified in the present collection). Fred Whitemore (Chapter 9) takes the story forward into the present century, by giving a valuable and informative account of the changing attitudes to democracy in the British Labour Party during the past hundred years or so. He charts very clearly how wider issues of economic and social democracy ceased to be active and central concerns in the labour movement, from the 1920s almost to the present day.

The last two contributions concentrate on aspects of the movement towards democracy in the communist world. Richard Sakwa (Chapter 10) gives a detailed and well-informed account of the recent debates in the Soviet Union about democracy. Until recently, these focused particularly on the idea of a participatory, Council form of democracy; but now, as he shows, attention is turning more towards the constitutional problems of liberal forms of democracy. Interestingly, Sakwa's account reveals the extent to which many of the issues which have concerned the left here are also central to the Soviet discussion. Finally, Peter Ferdinand (Chapter 11) describes the development of ideas about democracy in China. He analyses the background to the democracy movement which flowered so suddenly in Tiennanmen Square in 1989, and its brutal and tragic suppression by tanks and guns. He stresses the absence of a democratic tradition and political culture in China. In view of this, it should perhaps be seen as impressive evidence of the wide appeal of the idea of democracy that it has seized hold even there.

Right wing commentators have been proclaiming the death of socialism and the triumph of capitalism and liberal democracy. According to Fukuyama, we are witnessing the 'end of history'. Politics, he predicts, will lack diversity and become boring and predictable. On the evidence of these papers he could hardly be further from the truth. Their diversity, interest and liveliness suggest that recent events, in both West and East – the emergence of new social forces in the West, the crumbling of cold war divisions, the democratization in the communist world – are leading rather to a new beginning. They give every reason to hope that what is now in prospect is a period of revival and new development of creative thought and controversy on the left.

2 Democracy and the Idea of the Left

John Keane

What does it mean to be on the Left today? Few questions are so theoretically and politically significant – and so utterly perplexing. Only the origins of the term 'Left' seem uncontroversial.

It is well known that the idea of the Left is a child of the French Revolution – a metaphorical extension of the seating plan of the 1789 French Estates-General, which became divided by the heated debates on the royal veto, with the Third Estate sitting to the King's left and the nobility to his right. It is also common knowledge that the idea of the Left played a critical role in nineteenth century politics. It heightened the perception of the body politic as a broken continuum, as permanently divided by competing attitudes towards social change and political order. In opposition to the foot-dragging conservatism of the Right, with its haughty belief in the need for inequality, strict order and social control, and against the moderate liberal centre – the 'juste milieu' (Benjamin Constant) of limited monarchy and limited democracy – Leftists were progressives. They optimistically embraced a faith in science, rationality and industry. They proclaimed their love of liberty and equality, and appealed to the essential goodness and sociability of human nature. The Left sympathized with the downtrodden. It despised the rich and powerful. It often denounced parliamentary democracy as a bourgeois institution. It battled for a world freed from the evils of capitalism, was, material scarcity and unhappiness.

Since the First Word War this classical image of the Left has been crumbling slowly. The Left has become more cautious about modernity. It is less magnetized by the myths of scientific-technical progress and, especially within its green fringes, it has become openly hostile to industrialism; by contrast, it is the Right, from Mussolini to Thatcher, which has abandoned its former nostalgia and circumspection, and pressed home revolutionary or reformist policies based on a deep faith in scientific and economic modernization. In the same period, the levelling image of the Left has been damaged badly by its association with the cruel Stalinist programme of destroying liberty, equality and solidarity by means of cunning, violence, blood and terror – in Spain, the Moscow trials, the Hitler–Stalin pact, Katyn and the military invasions of Hungary and Czechoslovakia. In consequence, the Left has become widely identified with the mastery of the skills of the lion and the fox, with the passion for political power and the wholesale politicization of personal and social life.

The Left's founding image of international class solidarity and opposition to state violence has also taken a severe beating. The rise of national communist regimes (as in Yugoslavia, China and Vietnam) has demonstrated that Leftism is not synonymous with selfless internationalism. Severe tensions among these regimes – the Maoist denunciation of Soviet 'revisionism' as a right-wing betrayal of communism is a dramatic case in point – and the more recent outbreak of war between these states (as in Indo-China) have served to reinforce the image of the Left as a purveyor of self-interested power politics – as a mirror image of its right-wing opponents.

In recent years, the meaning of the term 'Left' has fallen into deeper disarray, especially in the countries of the West. It has become a muddled label which often obscures more than it clarifies. The appearance of the New Left at the end of the 1950s is one source of this trend. The willingness of many Left governments and parties after 1945 to embrace the 'mixed economy' and their more recent fascination with market mechanisms, the profit motive and small business has further blurred its distinctively 'Left' qualities. Matters have been worsened by the confused reaction of trade unions, once considered the 'natural' heartland of Left support, to the failure of Keynesian reflationary policies. This confusion has been multiplied by uncertainty about de-industrialization, the growth of a new underclass and the emergence of more 'flexible' technologies, production methods and consumer styles. The western Left's loss of direction can also be traced to its nostalgic defence of centralized state bureaucracy and outdated techniques of management and planning. The conventional belief on the Left that state planning and fixing of markets plus selective nationalization plus spending money equals socialism has come unstuck. And the consequent tendency of some parts of the Left to display more pride in the past than faith in the future has been exacerbated by its intellectual torpor – its bad habit of submitting to the hypnotic powers of the Right, of repeating clichés and making politics through conventional labels.

DEMOCRACY RETRIEVED

I see the demand for more democracy as the key to a successful redefinition of the Left – and therefore as the key to overcoming the confusion and self-contradictory orientations of the present-day Left. What does democracy mean in this context? The concept of democracy is not infinitely elastic. It is not a word which can be made to mean whatever we choose it to mean. Democracy is best understood as a system of procedural rules with normative implications. These rules specify *who* is authorized to make collective decisions and through which *procedures* such decisions are to be made. In contrast to all forms of heteronomous government, democracy comprises procedures for arriving at collective decisions in a way which secures the fullest possible and qualitatively best participation of interested parties. At a minimum – here the normative implications of my proceduralist definition of democracy become evident – democratic procedures include equal and universal adult suffrage; majority rule and guarantees of minority rights, which ensure that collective decisions are approved by a substantial number of those expected to make them; the rule of law; and constitutional guarantees of freedom of assembly and expression and other liberties, which help guarantee that those expected to decide, or to elect those who decide, can choose among real alternatives. It therefore requires – as I first argued in *Public Life and Late Capitalism* and specified more recently in *The Media and Democracy* – the institutional division of state and civil society; that is, the building of a type of multilayered (supranational) state which is held permanently accountable to a pluralistic, self-organizing (international) civil society, as well as mechanisms – political parties, parliaments, communications media and corporatist procedures – which openly mediate state and social institutions.

Democracy in this sense is a guarantee of pluralism. Its procedures function as the 'ground rules' of a system of complex equality, liberty and solidarity which makes room for a wide diversity of forms of life. That is why the attempt to redefine the Left as the democratic fight for more and better democracy takes care of the possible objection that the Left–Right distinction (and other binary opposites such as labour/capital, men/women and domestic/foreign) are obsolete because they are insufficiently subtle and therefore incapable of coming to terms with the sociological and ethical complexity of the late twentieth century world. To be a Leftist is to acknowledge and respect the complexity of our existence. It is to be on bad terms with the homogeneity and heteronomy of undemocratic institutions. It involves a permanent obligation actively to question every enforced consensus and extended silence. It is to work for greater diversity in the face of compulsory homogeneity and institutional standardization. Defined in this novel way, the Left can no longer be identified with the passion for political power. Democracy is a method of preventing those who govern from permanently appropriating power for their own ends. Those exercising power are subject to procedures which enable others to question, rotate or sack them. The distribution of power in democratic systems tends to reflect the outcomes of political contests framed by permanent decision-making rules. Conflict and compromise are therefore institutionalized, and power becomes secular and 'disembodied'. It is not permanently consubstantial with any particular individual or group – a monarch, for instance – but is exercised instead by flesh-and-blood mortals who are subject to removal and are accountable to others, in accordance with the rules of the democratic game.

MISCONCEPTIONS ABOUT DEMOCRACY

In my view, significant parts of the present-day Left have either muddled or no clear ideas about the importance and nature of the rules of democracy, and in particular whether to reform or replace them. We need to challenge several standard Leftist misconceptions about democracy. For example, it is clear that the historical emergence of liberal democratic institutions, such as free elections, competitive party systems and written constitutions, represented a great leap forward in the fight for more democracy. Liberal democratic institutions are not necessarily a device for protecting the class interests of the bourgeoisie. Liberal democracy (to paraphrase Lenin) is not the best political shell for capitalism. Liberal democratic institutions are in fact an indispensible bulwark against the unending arrogance of political actors, a vital mechanism for limiting the scope and haughtiness of state power. A post-liberal democracy is thinkable and desirable, but a non-liberal democracy is a contradiction in terms and in fact.

It also needs to be said that the friends of democracy must reject the bad 'New Left' habit of calling for the disappearance of all organization and its replacement by so-called spontaneous action. A democratic polity without procedural rules is not only a contradiction in terms. It is also a recipe for arbitrary decision-making and misgovernment. The friends of democracy must also recognize that the full replacement of representative forms of democracy by participatory, direct democracy – which require (in the case of decisions affecting the whole polity) the public assembly of millions of citizens – is technically impossible in large-scale, complex societies. Direct democracy, the participation of citizens in the *agora*, is suited only to small states and organizations in which 'the people find it easy to meet and in which every citizen can easily get to know all the others' (Rousseau). More controversially: the attempt to foist the principle of direct democracy on to representative institutions – for instance, applying a binding mandate to elected parliamentary 'delegates' – is undesirable, since it contradicts the principle, indispensible in any parliamentary democracy, that representatives represent general rather than narrowly sectional interests and therefore require some powers to negotiate freely and to act independently of those whom they represent.

The important point is that direct democracy thrives upon consensual decision-making, and that it therefore works best when there are a limited number of alternative policy choices – nuclear power or no nuclear power, peace or war, or the legalization or criminalization of abortion. Otherwise, the trust, patience and mutual support that are required within self-governing circles are often overburdened with multiple and conflicting points of view, the tensions among which cannot be resolved easily without the presence of intermediaries – that is, without institutions of delegated or represetnative democracy which 'filter out' and simplify the kaleidoscope of conflicting opinions.

This is not to say that representative, parliamentary democracy is the alpha and omega of political forms. In western countries the representative system is not only besieged by various undemocratic trends (such as the decline of legislatures, the growth of military and policing agencies and unrestricted government advertising). It is also constrained and limited by accumulations of *social* power within civil society. The vast majority of citizens has no say in major decisions concerning economic investment, production and growth. Churches, trade unions, the media and many other institutions of civil society remain insufficiently democratic. Exactly how more democracy within the sphere of civil society might be achieved in practice is a central theme of my *Democracy and Civil Society*. It argues for the extension of the process of democratization from the political sphere (where individuals are regarded as citizens) to the civil sphere, where there are multiple and conflicting identities, where individuals are regarded variously as men and women, entrepreneurs and workers, teachers and students, producers and consumers. Struggles over *where* citizens can vote should be given as much priority as the struggles in the nineteenth and early twentieth centuries over *who* can vote.

In practice this refinement and extension of democracy – broadening the domains *where* citizens can vote – does not require all individuals to play the role of full-time political animals. Too much democracy can kill off democracy. The wholesale politicization of life, the attempt to create a society of full-time, omnicompetent citizens, is in fact antithetical to democracy. It would produce hellish and unworkable results – everything would be defined as political, private life would be swallowed up by the public sphere, human beings would be transformed, perhaps forcibly, into 'total citizens', despite the fact that the growing diversification and complexity of modern societies prevents individual citizens from being present in the same place at the same time to make decisions which affect their lives directly or indirectly. Free time would become a thing of the past. The quality of decision-making would decline. The life of the full-time, omnicompetent citizen would be a nightmare of interminable meetings, endless negotiations and late-night telephone calls. Moreover, Europeans are heirs of an historical tradition in which state power is supposed to be limited in favour of non-state spheres, such as religious communities, households, centres of learning and research, and markets.

This historically felt need to limit the scope and power of the state – examined in my *Civil Society and the State* – was theorized by a wide variery of west European thinkers, from Burke and Hegel to Proudhon and Durkheim. Today it must be a central and distinctive feature of the attempt to redefine the meaning of Left politics. State power is necessary and yet corruptible and dangerous, and it is therefore in need of preventive measures and effective defences, such as a plurality of social forces and organizations which run parallel to the state. The enormous problem which faces the Left is to know how to create through its own agency a state apparatus which is efficient without being oppressive or, in other words, which can function effectively as the agent of civil society without at the same time lapsing into a dictatorship.

But there is another key task of contemporary democratic theory: to explore the limitations or weaknesses of democracy, to recognize that democracy cannot achieve certain things, and that there are ways in which it tends to undermine itself. There are quite a number of weaknesses inherent in the democratic method. Consider two examples. Democracy's lack of philosophical self-confidence is among the most obvious. In a famous aphorism, Novalis pointed out that philosophy is required to explain itself. This aphorism applies equally to contemporary democratic theory, which is slowly waking from an extended period of inebriated merrymaking. Democratic ideals nowadays resemble a homeless drunk staggering uncertainly in search of a lamp-post for support, if not illumination. This was not always so. For the past two centuries democratic thinkers in Europe and elsewhere have typically attempted to justify democracy by referring back to a subtantive grounding principle. There are many cases that can be cited: the belief of Mazzini and others that the growth of democracy is a Law of History; the argument of Tom Paine, Georg Forster and others that democracy is grounded in the natural rights of citizens; the Benthamite assumption that democracy is an implied condition of the principle of utility; the belief of Theodor Parker and others that democracy is a form of government based on the principle of eternal justice, on the unchanging law of God; and the (Marxian) claim that the triumph of authentic democracy is dependent upon the world-historical struggle of the proletariat. Belief in these various first principles has today crumbled, and that is why democracy is no longer understandable as a self-evidently desirable set of procedural norms. Democracy is now suffering a permanent legitimation crisis. A genuine philosophy of democracy cannot become a universal language, capable of knowing everything, refuting all its opponents and concretely synthesising all differences. For this reason democracy is presently vulnerable to its fundamentalist critics, who preach the teaching of Allah, the Rule of Law, class struggle or some other substantive principle. Philosophical insecurity is the quintessential feature of the contemporary democratic identity.

A second type of weakness of the democratic method is the inability of democratic procedures to resolve the tense relationship between socio-political institutions and the natural environment within which they are forced to operate. At the close of the twentieth century the human species is ever more bent on interfering with and controlling its natural environment. We even have developed the nuclear capacity to destroy ourselves and outer nature. This is why, in recent years, there has been widespread public reaffirmation of the point that human beings are but one element within a wider, highly complex ecosystem, and that we have an obligation to act responsibly towards nature. Hence the dilemma between the growing power of humans to manipulate and control nature and the growing need of the human species to give institutional recognition to our fundamental dependence upon nature. This dilemma cannot be resolved by democratic means. In contrast to systems of despotic power, democracies are certainly capable of fostering public awareness of this dilemma. But they cannot overcome it. Democracies cannot become full masters and possessors of nature (in the sense of Bacon). But – if they wish to maintain the public controversy and openness to new ideas which are among their central features – democracies cannot 'return to nature'. They can neither be absolutely artificial nor absolutely natural. They can at best recognize this dilemma, acknowledging that it cannot be overcome by democracy itself.

The friends of democracy need urgently to discuss these types of problems, if only to defend democracy against its harshest critics. Admittedly, this is a controversial undertaking. For over two millenia political thinkers have insisted upon the chaos of democratic politics, the decadence of democratic constitutions and the moral depravity of the democratic character. Reacting against this anti-democratic tradition, some contemporary democrats insist that to interrogate the democratic method is to erode its credibility and to destroy its self-confidence. This conviction is mistaken. The long-term survival of democracy must involve anticipating the objections of its critics, honestly exploring the dilemmas and paradoxes which riddle democratic politics, thereby recognizing that democracy cannot achieve certain things. Democratic theory must state issues it knows it cannot resolve; it must attempt to hold up a mirror, admittedly somewhat misted, to look at itself in. The democratic method has clear limits, which should serve as a warning against attempts to build a perfect democracy. Like the behaviour of the daughters of Pelia, who tried to rejuvenate their ageing father by hacking him to pieces, attempts to perfect democracy endanger democracy itself.

WHY DEMOCRACY?

Even though democracy has endemic limits, it remains superior to all other dictatorial methods of decision-making. Why sympathize with the democratic method – especially considering the fact that in the history of political thought democracy has had many more enemies than friends? Why consider the democratization of the Left – its unconditional embrace of the democratic method – of paramount importance? In short, why is democracy a good thing?

In *Public Life and Late Capitalism* I argued (against Habermas and others) that democracy should not be considered as a type of normative (or, as Kant would say, imperative) language game, and that – here I followed a clue provided by Hans Kelsen's *Vom Wesen und Wert der Demokratie* – it is best understood as an implied condition and practical consequence of philosophical and political pluralism. The separation of civil society from the state, as well as the democratization of each – a post-capitalist civil society guarded by a democratic state – are necessary conditions for enabling a genuine plurality of individuals and groups openly to express their solidarity with (or opposition to) others' ideals and forms of life. Understood in this new way, the concept of democratization abandons the futile search for definite Truths and safe highroads of human existence. It makes it possible at last for us to live without the indefensible ideological concepts – Order, Progress, History, Humanity, Nature, Socialism, Individualism, Nation, Sovereignty of the People – upon which the early modern advocates of democracy based their claims for greater equality and freedom.

This non-foundationalist understanding of democracy requires further elaboration. It certainly needs to extend the frontiers of the democratic imagination by providing new and undogmatic arguments for the superiority of the democratic method. Consider the following example. It is often said that the most important feature of democratic procedures is that they enable the approval of decisions of interest to the whole collectivity, or at least a majority of citizens. This overlooks the key point – still inadequately recognized in democratic theory – that democratic procedures also enable the *disapproval* and *revision* of established agreements, and that for this reason they are uniquely suited to complex western societies. Democratic procedures are superior to all other types of decision-making not because they guarantee both a consensus and 'good' decisions, but because they provide citizens who are affected by certain decisions with the possibility of reconsidering their judgements about the quality and unintended consequences of these decisions. Democratic procedures increase the level of 'flexibility' and 'reversibility' of decision-making. They encourage incremental learning and trial-and-error modification (or 'muddling through'), and that is why they are best suited to the task of publicly monitoring and controlling (and sometimes shutting down) complex and tightly coupled 'high-risk' organizations, whose failure (as in Bhopal, Three-Mile Island and Chernobyl) can have catastrophic ecological and social consequences. Democracy is an unrivalled remedy for technocratic delusions. It is an indispensible means of making accountable those who turn a blind eye to the 'normal accidents' which plague high-risk systems, and who seek to define acceptable levels of risk by means of technical analyses of probability – or simply by falling back on the childish solipsism that whatever isn't believed couldn't possibly be harmful.

Only democratic procedures can openly and fairly select certain kinds of dangers for public attention, carefully monitor and bring to heel those responsible for managing risky organizations, thereby minimizing the possibility of error and reducing the chances of the big mistake. Unfortunately, most contemporary democratic theory does not consider this unusual line of reasoning. A new theory of democracy needs to pursue this path. At the same time, it must engage with the more conventional types of arguments for democracy. The first and weakest of these is the utilitarian argument that democracy is superior to dictatorship because it enables the best interpreters of interests – the interested parties themselves – to sift through various options and to decide for themselves. Aside from the probability that interested individuals and groups confuse their short-term and longer-run interests because they often see no further than their own noses, the utilitarian argument mistakenly assumes that the collective interest is only ever the sum of individual interests. A second and more convincing type of argument is that democratic procedures maximize freedom in the sense of autonomy. Why autonomy is a good thing is unclear from most of these accounts. They simply assume that it one of those ultimate values which cannot be deduced rationally. If freedom (to paraphrase Rousseau) is obedience to the laws which citizens formulate and apply to themselves then democratic procedures for arriving at collective decisions through the fullest possible participation of interested parties is a natural ally of autonomy.

Finally consideration must be given to the view that democracy is superior because it remains the strongest antidote to the abuse of power. Montesquieu, Madison and others were correct: those who exercise power always want more of it and for more extended periods. A bad democracy is for this reason always better than a good dictatorship. Democracy is a self-reflexive means of controlling the exercise of power, and it is for this reason an indispensible weapon in

the fight to question, restrict and to dissolve dictatorial power. Democrats are certainly not exempted from this democratic equation. Democrats seek to alter radically and to equalize the existing distribution of power within and between the state and civil society. They are normally confronted with various acts of sabotage and resistance by their opponents and, hence, faced with the temptation of overcoming such obstacles by accumulating ever more power. The lust for power knows no political affiliation. It is polymorphously perverse. It requires constant correction and eternal vigilance.

SOCIALISM

This rule applies especially to those who consider themselves as heirs to a socialist version of the classical Left project. In capitalist society – according to Marx and others – the institutional bases of class power and state power are differentiated. The separation of political and social forms of stratification is seen (correctly) to be a unique feature of the modern bourgeois era. The human species is subdivided for the first time into *social* classes; individuals' legal status is divorced from their socio-economic role within civil society; each individual is sundered into both private egoist and public-spirited citizen; and civil society, the realm of private needs and interests, waged labour and private right, is emancipated from political control, and becomes the basis and presupposition of the state. Civil society is also the power base of the leading class, the bourgeoisie, which is the first 'non-political' class in human history. Its control of civil society ensures that political power is normally a secondary or derivative phenomenon; the state is an instrument for protecting and managing the political affairs of the bourgeoisie and its allies.

From the time of its birth in the 1820s, the socialist project aimed to undo this development by abolishing the social power of the bourgeoisie and, hence, by destroying the division between civil society and the state. The problem, analyzed in depth in *Democracy and Civil Society*, is that state power tends to become dictatorial whenever it ceases to be subject to the countervailing powers of civil society. And that is not the only problem. If socialism means a society in which ownership of the means of production has been transferred from private hands into the laps of 'society' – in the twentieth century that has normally meant the state itself – then the abuses of state power are (and have been) much more likely than in a capitalist society. Under socialist conditions, citizens would be exposed constantly to the whims and calculations of a state which simultaneously performs the functions of policeman, administrator, social worker *and* employer.

The demand for socialism in this sense is undemocratic. The demand for democracy is much more subversive because it calls into question all heternomous forms of power. This is why the democratization of the Left, its militant defence of the democratic method, is of fundamental contemporary importance. The Left needs democracy in order to live up to its old promises of greater equality and solidarity *with* liberty; but in view of the systematic failure of the Left to keep these promises, its full acceptance of the democratic method would radically alter the methods, policies and public image of the Left. It would become a synonym for the democratic fight for greater democracy.

While this proposed redefinition of the Left is tentative and its policy implications sketchy, its deep political significance should not be underestimated. Once or twice in each century whole political spectrums break up and undergo massive realignment. We are living through one of these painful and topsy-turvy periods of readjustment, and the revised understanding of democracy sketched in these notes helps to explain why. It exposes several key blindspots and muddles of the Left. It helps to clarify the advantages and disadvantages of the democratic method. It deepens our understanding of the collapse of the communist project and heightens our appreciation of the unexpected global upsurge of the democratic revolution at the end of the twentieth century – in Poland and Hungary, Czechoslovakia and the DDR, Brazil and Argentina, the Philippines and China. The arguments summarized here will nevertheless irritate many orthodox Leftists, especially those who continue to defend the primacy of 'socialism' and who consequently fail to see that the citizen has problems distinct from those of the worker or consumer, and that political and social democracy cannot be resolved into economic democracy. For those who remain flippant about the advantages of democracy, or who turn a blind eye to the ways in which contemporary western democracies are fragile, corruptible and often corrupt – those who haven't yet seen that the middle of the political road is often a dead end – the redefinition of democracy should be disturbing. And for smug neo-conservatives, who pronounce the death of the Left by implosion, this redefinition should serve as a warning that the imagination of a new democratic Left has begun to stir.

3 Socialism, Radical Democracy, and Class Politics

Andrew Gamble

The relationship between socialism and democracy has always been controversial. Alexander Solzhenitsyn once declared the idea of socialist democracy to be as meaningful as boiling ice. Milton Friedman has argued that capitalism is a necessary condition for democracy,[1] while for Irving Kristol and Daniel Bell the exposure of socialism to democracy has produced the death of socialism.[2] By this they mean not just the failure of socialist societies to deliver democracy and prosperity, but the collapse of belief in the possibility and even the desirability of socialism.

Socialists however remain obstinately attached to the idea that socialism and democracy are strongly related. Nicos Poulantzas wrote at the end of his last book: 'One thing is certain: Socialism will be democratic or it will not be at all'.[3] A major change of emphasis is apparent in the priority socialists now give to democracy. Formerly socialists chose to emphasise that without socialism there could be no democracy. Now like Poulantzas most socialists believe that without democracy there can be no socialism.

The historical connection between socialism and democracy is very close. Socialists took the lead in pressing for the extension of full citizenship rights including the vote to all citizens. Liberals and Conservatives were either sceptical or opposed to the rise of democracy and predicted dire consequences for the security of property. Democracy was seen to be a political system in which the poor would acquire the means to plunder the rich, or in which the views and tastes of the ignorant would prevail over those of the educated.

The fight for democracy and the fight for socialism often seemed to be the same fight. Democracy meant placing political power in the hands of the people, wresting it away from the owners of property. The demand for universal suffrage was a demand simultaneously for the introduction of socialism. Supporters and opponents of democracy believed that if the vote were extended to all, socialism would be its inevitable outcome. Marx appears to have expected this also when he declared that the achievement of universal suffrage in a country like England, where the workers had a majority, would inevitably mean the political supremacy of the working class. Many of the early Marxist parties called themselves Social Democratic parties. Their fight was against political absolutism as well as capitalism. If the bourgeoisie's monopoly of state power could be broken the way would be open for the triumph of socialism.

One hundred years later the association between socialism and democracy is no longer so evident. Democracy has been appropriated by conservatism and liberalism, and some of the most striking democratic revolutions at the end of the twentieth century have taken place against the state socialist regimes of the communist bloc. The argument of the nineteenth century has been turned on its head. Then it was alleged that democracy threatened to instal political forces which would destroy the basis for economic liberty. Now it is asserted that only the institutions of economic liberty, specifically private property and markets, can ensure the survival of democracy. Governments that fail to understand the nature of this link risk both economic prosperity and the continuance of democracy.

The reasons for the weakening of the association between socialism and democracy in the twentieth century are complex. The split in the ranks of social democracy between Communists and Socialists after 1917 was in part a split over the priority that should be attached to democratic institutions and methods. The social democratic parties became strongly committed to the preservation of democracy, while the Communist regimes became identified with the building of a socialist economic and social system and the suppression of representative institutions. The Communist states failed to achieve democracy while the social democratic parties failed to inaugurate socialism.

During the twentieth century socialism has not been achieved anywhere through democratic means. Social democratic parties even when they have won power have not succeeded in establishing socialism. Communist parties where they have seized state power have abolished capitalism but at the expense of repressing all opposition. Where socialism has been successful democracy has been absent. Where democracy has flourished socialism has been rejected.

In these circumstances it is hardly surprising that the crumbling of communist power throughout the eastern bloc should have been accompanied by renewed claims that ideology and even history are now coming to an end with the final triumph of liberal democracy and the defeat of socialism. So firm is the Right's appropriation of democracy that the final synthesis is termed 'liberal democracy' rather than liberal capitalism.

Socialists naturally contest the way in which democracy is now defined and the serious lacunae in the theory of the end of history.[4] Almost all socialists have long dissociated themselves from the corrupt, inefficient, and oppressive regimes of the Communist bloc. But this does not solve the basic problem. Socialists are forced to acknowledge that there is no example of a successful transition to socialism through democratic institutions. Socialist economies have been established only where democratic institutions either did not exist or were rapidly destroyed. These economies have also turned out to offer no viable basis for organising a successful industrial society. In most of the state socialist countries there has been a substantial retreat from the methods of central planning towards the reintroduction not just of the market but private property as well.

CLASS POLITICS

The failure of both social democracy and state socialism to develop a viable model of socialism casts doubts on the socialist project. What grounds exist for continuing to believe that a socialist future is either possible or desirable?

The response from the mainstream Marxist tradition has been to reject both the state socialism of the East and the social democracy of the West and to insist that there is a viable alternative to both. The idea of democracy through workers' councils is offered as a third way which bypasses the representative institutions of liberal democracy as well as avoiding the bureaucracy of centralised state power. Although workers' councils do not exclude some types of representation, the emphasis is on forms of direct democracy in which all participate in the formation of the collective will and the taking of collective decisions. Representatives are delegates, strictly accountable to their electors.

The experience of workers' councils has been limited. They have sprung up during revolutionary periods in Russia, in Italy, and in Hungary. But they have tended to be short-lived, and have never had an extended trial. They are put forward as the solution to the inadequate democracy of parliamentary regimes and the absence of democracy in bureaucratic regimes.

What lies behind the endorsement of council democracy by socialists are two key ideas in the Marxist tradition – firstly about the nature of politics and secondly about the future classless society. The first idea is the belief that it is possible to create a political community in which the duties of individuals as citizens are paramount. Their public selves are more important than their private selves. The public realm is the sphere of action and of honour. Individuals realise their highest potential by participating in the collective deliberations of their community.

This image of the good society has at times been confused by assertions that under socialism public affairs would lose their political character. What was being rejected however was the idea of politics as relationships of domination and subordination. It was to be superseded by politics as participation and community. The clear implication in classical Marxist texts is that once classes have been abolished there would be no relationships of power or social conflicts that could not be handled through the institutional mechanisms of a democracy in which all citizens were full participants.

The second idea is the claim that in a socialist society there would be steady progress towards the elimination of private property and commodity production. Markets would increasingly be replaced until the stage of full communism was reached. The goal of socialism is defined as the creation of a society of associated producers, a society without markets and without classes, in which the purpose of production is the direct satisfaction of human needs. The decisions of what to produce and how to allocate resources and organize production would be taken not through markets and competition or by experts and bureaucracies but through a process of collective decision-making in which all the producers have an equal voice.

The concept of the society of associated producers has to imply this kind of participatory democracy if it is not to mean simply authoritative allocation through bureaucratic agencies in place of competitive markets. Far from withering away, the role of politics would actually be immense in such a society. All economic decisions would have been politicized. In Hirschman's terms the opportunities for exit would have been greatly reduced in favour of increasing the opportunities for voice.[5] The insistence in classical Marxism that there would be no need for politics and for the state derives from the identification of these terms with the institutions of a class society. The socialist revolution transforms the state by ending the separation of state and civil society. The associated producers create a true political community by forging a genuine collective will which determines all major issues.

Full Communism is the socialist version of the end of history. For once classes have been abolished there is no longer any reason for the existence of political parties. There are no issues that involve fundamental conflict. There will still be conflicts, but these can be resolved peacefully by a process of public discussion which arrives at a consensus that everyone can accept. Once a classless society has been achieved, there are problems of adjustment and coordination, but these are essentially administrative problems, not political and ideological problems in the old sense.

LIBERAL DEMOCRACY

This view of the relationship between socialism and democracy continues the classical Marxist tradition, and sets out an apparent third way between social democracy and state socialism. Its main weakness is its utopian character. There is no society in the world that closely approximates such a society, and there is no longer any clear mechanism as to how such a society might be brought about in the future. Classical Marxism had such influence on socialist thinking because it combined an analysis of the way in which capitalist societies were developing with a clear specification of the agency by which these societies would be transformed.

Classical Marxism now finds itself under attack. Some of the fiercest questioning has centred on its assumptions about socialism and democracy. Its critics range from leading democratic socialists like Noberto Bobbio and Michael Walzer to the new post-Marxist school which has become particularly well-established in Britain. Its representatives include Ernesto Laclau and Chantal Mouffe, Barry Hindess and Paul Hirst. There is also an important stream influenced by Gramsci which includes Stuart Hall, Alan Hunt, Bob Jessop and John Keane.

What is emerging out of all the current writing on the relationship between socialism and democracy is a concept of radical democracy which is distinct both from traditional social democracy and state socialism, but also embodies a sharp critique of the conception of council democracy. It thus embodies a far-reaching critique of socialist and Marxist theory with a specification of a new political strategy for achieving socialism.

The advocates of radical democracy have received a vigorous response from those who wish to retain the fundamental elements of the Marxist tradition. They emphasize the continuing importance and relevance of class politics, both for understanding contemporary capitalism and for deriving a strategy for moving towards socialism. Two key contributions to this complex and extensive debate will be discussed here – firstly the liberal socialism of Noberto Bobbio, and secondly the post-Marxism of Laclau and Mouffe.

Noberto Bobbio is an acute critic both of the assumptions of classical Marxism and of the political practice of Marxist parties in particular the PCI.[6] His main target is what he sees as the persistent failure of Marxism to take democracy seriously. By democracy Bobbio means representative democracy, which is the only kind of democracy which he thinks has any substance. The bias of Marxism has been to undervalue the importance of formal democratic institutions by treating them instrumentally and forecasting their disappearance under socialism. For many socialists, for example, the importance of democracy lies in the greater scope that it provides for the organization of the working class to struggle against capialism. Parliaments are seen as important not in their own right but only in so far as they provide a forum for exposing the injustices of the capitalist order.

Bobbio traces this attitude to Marx. By treating all states as class dictatorships Marx established a method that many of his followers used in the era of mass democracy to deny the legitimacy of democratic institutions. This method was closely linked to the belief in the possibility of creating a classless society after the revolution. It was guaranteed by the epistemological claim that Marxism alone among political analyses could claim scientific objectivity. It had a number of other consequences, among them the dismissal of political argument based on individual rights as a conception belonging to the bourgeois era, which would be superseded once the transition to socialism had been successfully accomplished.

Bobbio argues that assumptions of this kind make it very difficult for Marxism to develop a successful democratic politics. It never takes democracy seriously enough because its attitude towards democracy is always instrumental. Marxists are continually looking beyond democracy to a society where this form of democracy will not exist.

This attitude is rooted in the Marxist doctrine of the relationship between the economic base and the political superstructure. What Bobbio and many other socialists following Gramsci now question is the interpretation of civil society which Marx adopted from Hegel. When Marx declared that the key to understanding the state lay in civil society and that the anatomy of civil society was to be found in political economy, he identified the class character of civil society, specifically the institution of private property, as the basis of the capitalist state. This perspective was both liberating and constricting. It widened the context in which politics had to be understood, but it also tended to reduce all other manifestations of politics to a class basis.

Such an approach ignored the complexity of civil society by identifying it so closely with the conception of commercial society developed by the Scottish political economists. It was left to other political traditions to analyse civil society as an arena with relative independence from both the state and capital. Civil society as a network of institutions, associations, pressure groups, communication media, political movements and political parties came to be seen both as the main defence against state despotism, and of the main source of ideas of citizenship, justice and liberty.

The importance of Gramsci for Bobbio is that he rediscovered the significance of civil society for a socialist politics. Bobbio argues that Gramsci's thought still remained embedded in classical Marxist assumptions, but that even if he never broke entirely with the classical Marxist explanation of the relationship between base and superstructure, he did shift Marxist thought towards an examination of the importance of analysing the relative autonomy of the superstructure.

Bobbio wants to go much further. For him the only feasible socialist politics is a politics that makes the protection of democratic institutions its first priority. If socialists do not make the commitment socialism risks degenerating into dictatorship. As Bobbio puts it:

> a dictatorship, even one with the trappings of socialism, never achieves anything more, as far as the mass of the population who has to endure it is concerned, than a change in the ruling élite.[7]

What he also disputes however is that the alternative of council democracy, which the classical Marxist tradition counterposes to bureaucratic dictatorship, is any alternative at all. He writes a fierce critique of the feasibility of any form of direct democracy in the conditions of modern industrial societies. For reasons of scale, complexity, and imperfect knowledge, forms of direct democracy cannot hope to cope with the problems of administering a modern state. Decision-making through small-scale political communities is only possible either for short periods in times of crisis and emergency, or for well-defined and minor problems. The extent of interdependence in modern societies makes it highly unsuitable for reaching decisions that will affect the whole society. The pretence that it might becomes the cloak behind which a centralised dictatorship assumes power.

Bobbio's critique of council democracy has similarities with that of Max Weber and also with the tradition of élite theory represented by Pareto and Mosca. It runs in harness with the critique of the feasibility of a socialist economy without markets. The connection between markets and the flourishing civil society have often been noted. The belief that representative democracy can be abandoned and that markets can be eradicated as a method of allocating resources and coordinating production in modern industrial societies are seen as illusions that only prepare the way for bureaucratic state socialism of the kind established throughout east and central Europe by Stalinism.

Bobbio has no illusions about liberal democracy either however. He turns the same searchlight on to its shortcomings. He sets out four paradoxes of democracy, which prevent it achieving what democrats expect. As the optimum method for making collective decisions democracy has four enemies – the large-scale of modern life, the increasing bureaucratization of the state apparatus, the growing technicality of the decisions it is necessary to make, and the trend of civil society towards becoming a mass society.[8] He is therefore pessimistic about the prospects of achieving progress towards socialism through democratic institutions. But he argues that, mediocre although contemporary democracy may be, it is at least much better than any form of dictatorship, whether of the fascist or the state socialist kind.

For Bobbio democracy despite its faults is preferable to other forms of government. There are ethical, political, and utilitarian arguments in its favour. It makes government depend on the freely expressed wishes of individual citizens, it gives some protection from abuses of power, and it makes the people the ultimate arbiters of what is in the public interest.

Limited although the case for democracy may be, Bobbio nevertheless regards the establishment of democratic institutions as the basic condition for any advance towards socialism. In this way the achievement of socialism becomes dependent on the extension of democracy – socialism is a part of the struggle for democracy rather than democracy a part of the struggle for socialism. Bobbio has no confidence that socialism will be ever achieved. He explicitly states that 'majority decisions in a political order based on universal suffrage permit changes *in* the system but they do not allow a change *of* the system'.[9] He acknowledges that the existence of private property in the means of production is a major obstacle to the achievement of socialism. His only suggestion for countering it is through the extension of economic democracy. But he acknowledges that any such structural reforms are bound to lead to resistance on the part of the owners of capital and can only be pressed so far without risking such dislocation and political turmoil that they would have to be abandoned. As Perry Anderson points out, Bobbio's suggestion that the question of who holds power is less important than how power is exercised directs attention away from the class constraints on policy to the institutional character of the regime.[10] Bobbio would respond however that historically there is no alternative.

RADICAL DEMOCRACY

Bobbio's view that socialism is part of the democratic project, a continuation of liberalism rather than a sharp break with it, is an emphasis shared by many of the post-Marxists. Ernesto Laclau and Chantal Mouffe have provided the most systematic and the boldest sketch of a post-Marxist politics.[11] Their conception of a socialist strategy presupposes the existence of democratic institutions.

Laclau and Mouffe argue that classical Marxism is mistaken in holding that the working class occupies a privileged position in the struggle for socialism. They condemn as 'essentialist' any attempt to identify structures that determine political events. Marx only succeeded in partially breaking with idealism. He succeeded in demonstrating that the meaning of any human reality is derived from a world of social relations that is broader than had previously been recognized. But he continued to conceive the relational logic linking the various spheres of social life in essentialist and idealist terms. The relationship Marx posits between economic base and political superstructure is for Laclau and Mouffe the core doctrine of Marxism. What they reject is the idea that any level always determines any other. What exists instead are phenomena related in a variety of ways, and which need to be understood as 'historical, contingent and constructed'.

If Marxism's claim to be an objective science of society is dropped, and if as a result Marxists abandon the attempt to identify which structures are determining structures in a social formation, then a politics is created which lacks any guarantees. There is no longer any guarantee that the working class occupies the key position in society, or that its location in the capitalist division of labour gives rise to a radical politics. There is no guarantee that the development of capitalism will either enlarge the working class, immiserate the working class, or make the working class revolutionary. There is no guarantee that capitalism will be succeeded by socialism.

Many of these guarantees have long been abandoned by most Marxists, but Laclau and Mouffe provide a reminder that the assumptions that underpinned them linger on. They argue that until Marxists break free of them they will remain wedded to a socialist strategy which is increasingly anachronistic, because it insists that everything must be built around the leading position of the working class.

Laclau and Mouffe offer instead an account of hegemony which emphasizes the need to forge links between a variety of independent social movements, in which no single movement can claim the leading role. Such a hegemonic project is an attempt to reflect the conditions of an increasingly open and pluralistic civil society. Its objective is to achieve a collective will of all the popular forces struggling to extend democracy.

The project for a radical democracy is therefore a project which includes socialism. Socialist demands and struggles are an important component but still only one component of the attempt to extend and deepen democracy. Laclau and Mouffe see the extension of democracy as the true revolution of modern times. Following Tocqueville they see this democratic revolution inaugurated by the events of the French Revolution spreading to affect all societies. Once the principle of equality is abroad, then sooner or later it is extended to all spheres of social life. Struggles against oppression and exploitation are different aspects of the general struggle for democratic rights.

Socialism becomes entirely subordinated to this concept of the democratic revolution. For Alan Hunt the goal of socialism is to complete the democratic revolution. Representative democracy, he argues, not only provides the best political framework for the transition to socialism but is an essential precondition for the political organization of the socialist society.[12]

Unlike Bobbio many of the post-Marxists exude political optimism. Laclau and Mouffe argue that the democratic movement is only now reaching maturity. The materialist programme can be reformulated in a much more radical way than was possible for Marx. They dismiss the idea that democratic politics means the creation of conformist and integrated societies. On the contrary democracy is seen as subversive of existing relationships of domination and oppression. The scope that still exists for pressing democratization further remains very great in capitalist societies. What has been lacking is the emergence of a radical anti-capitalist politics that is sufficiently broad to challenge existing concentrations of power. The fragmentation of radical democratic politics into different movements and the attempt by labour movements to be dominant rather than hegemonic has weakened the struggle against the established order. The merging of the concerns and objectives of socialists into a broader struggle to extend democracy makes possible an agenda of radical reform.

CONCLUSION

The idea of radical democracy has been criticized by those who still see class politics as the foundation of socialist politics. In many cases, however, such as that of Ellen Meiksins Wood's recent vigorous defence of a class politics perspective, *The Retreat From Class*, the tactic has been simply to restate the basic postulates of the Marxist approach.[13] The difficulty for Marxists is that such restatements do not address any of the current problems they face. The relationship between socialism and democracy is made a matter of definition. There is no recognition of how problematic the history of social democracy on the one hand and state socialism on the other have made that relationship. The first appears to offer the Left democracy without socialism, the second socialism without democracy. The response from classical Marxists is that neither represents true socialism. But that falls into the same utopian trap of which Ellen Meiksins Wood accuses the post-Marxists.

The proponents of liberal democracy and radical democracy have their own problems however. Anderson points out that ultimately Bobbio endorses liberalism. Only a modified liberalism appears possible given his pessimistic assessment of the possibilities of transforming advanced industrial societies. We are stuck in the iron cage and all we can hope to do is make it as comfortable and humane as possible. Przeworski says something very similar – the achievement of full employment, equality, and efficiency through the liberal democratic institutions of modern capitalism may be a second best but the best that is possible.[14]

Laclau and Mouffe and many of the post-Marxists have much broader ambitions than this. What is most valuable in their approach is the idea that the articulation between socialism and democracy is not an axiom but a political project, a long and complex hegemonic construction. What has disturbed their critics is how sweeping is their condemnation of classical Marxism, and how flimsy and rudderless is the radical democratic politics they are proposing. In order to give it some coherence they still have to draw on the concept of socialism and the socialist tradition. Indeed if this were not so it seems hard to see in what sense they could still claim to be socialist at all. If socialism still retains some meaning then the objective of widening the scope of non-commodity forms and ending the private ownership of the means of production have to be retained. The difficulty for socialists is whether these objectives still have plausibility. The class analysis of capitalism has not lost its power to provide insights into the way capitalism is developing. But the political hopes and strategies associated with it have proved illusory. The transformation of the fragmented working class into a class-for-itself in the classical Marxist concept is a very long way from being realised. Even great industrial struggles like the British Miners' strike of 1984/5 offer no support to the idea that a united class movement against capitalism is likely to emerge. It belongs to the past of the labour movement rather than to its future. From the perspective of the radical democracy theorists it was a defensive action by a sectional interest which failed to win active support from other groups of workers.

A socialism however without a workers' movement, without class analysis and class politics would hardly be a socialism at all. It would become just another variant of liberalism. This may be socialism's fate, lingering on as a critique of the shortcomings of liberalism, and as an analysis of the destructive effects of capitalist economics on individuals and communities. But there is another possibility. The waning of belief in the methods and politics of state socialism makes possible the intellectual and political rebirth of the socialist project by setting free once more hopes of emancipation.

If there is to be a rebirth the rediscovery of the importance of the political and of democracy will be central to it. The collapse of the regimes of state socialism makes social democracy once more the undisputed framework for socialist politics, but poses searching questions. Socialists cannot assume any longer that socialism and democracy go hand in hand. It has to be demonstrated. The really testing time for the relevance of socialism to the modern world may only just be beginning.

NOTES

1. Milton Friedman, *Capitalism and Freedom* (Chicago: University of Chicago Press, 1962).
2. Daniel Bell, *The End of Ideology: On the Exhaustion of Political Ideas in the 1950s* (Glencoe, Illinois: Free Press, 1960); Irving Kristol, *Two Cheers for Capitalism* (New York: Basic Books, 1978).
3. Nicos Poulantzas, *State, Power, Socialism* (London: New Left Books, 1978), p. 265.
4. Francis Fukuyama, 'The End of History', *The National Interest*, Summer 1989. For criticisms of Fukuyama's argument see the reviews by Gareth Stedman Jones, Edward Mortimer, and Jonathan Steele in *Marxism Today*, November 1989.
5. Albert Hirschman, *Exit, Voice, and Loyalty* (Cambridge, Mass.: Harvard University Press, 1970).
6. Noberto Bobbio, *Which Socialism? Marxism, Socialism, and Democracy* (Cambridge: Polity, 1987).
7. Bobbio, *Which Socialism?*, p. 87.
8. Ibid., p. 99.
9. Quoted in Perry Anderson, 'The Affinities of Norberto Bobbio', *New Left Review* 170, 1988, p. 32.
10. Perry Anderson, 'The Affinities of Noberto Bobbio', *New Left Review* 170, 1988, pp. 3–36.
11. Ernesto Laclau and Chantal Mouffe, *Hegemony and Socialist Strategy* (London: Verso, 1985).
12. Alan Hunt (ed.), *Marxism and Democracy* (London: Lawrence and Wishart, 1980).

13. Ellen Meiskins Wood, *The Retreat From Class* (London: Verso, 1986). For a discussion see Andrew Gamble, 'Class Politics and Radical Democracy', *New Left Review* 164 (1987), pp. 113–122.
14. Adam Przeworski, *Capitalism and Social Democracy* (Cambridge: Cambridge University Press, 1985).

4 Liberals versus Socialists: Who are the True Democrats?

John Hoffman

Since the Second World War ideologists of the liberal right have found it tempting to claim the mantle of democracy for themselves. Mrs Thatcher's recent declaration that British Tories are the true 'pioneers of world revolution' (1989, p. 6) is premissed on the assumption that democracy is synonymous with free enterprise – that it is only possible under a system of capitalism.

Socialists in general and Marxists in particular have frequently inverted the argument. Democracy under capitalism, they say, is truncated, formal and false. Only under socialism is real democracy possible. With characteristic flair, Michael Foot once wrote: 'the ideas of socialism and democracy, like liberty, equality and fraternity, came into the world joined together, and woe to those who would put them asunder' (1979, p. 17).

LIBERALS AS CRITICS OF DEMOCRACY: THE HISTORICAL ARGUMENT

A positive evaluation of democracy from all sides of the political spectrum is, as I have noted elsewhere (1988, pp. 132–3), a relatively recent phenomenon. In the nineteenth century T. D. Weldon's contention that 'democracy', 'liberalism' and 'capitalism' are simply different words for the same thing (1953, p. 86) would certainly have raised eyebrows, and in the eighteenth century liberal opposition to democracy was commonplace. Even the American republicans whom Tocqueville identified as introducing democracy in the New World looked upon the concept with a distinctly qualified enthusiasm.

When Madison argued that democrats would wickedly sponsor 'projects' like the abolition of debt or the use of paper money (Hamilton et al., pp. 81, 84), he was assuming, as the ancients did, that democracy was government by the poor – a system which, in

Rousseau's words, rested upon 'a large measure of equality in rank and fortune' (1968, p. 113). Give the propertyless the vote, Lord Macaulay warned James Mill in 1829, and the rich will be as mercilessly pillaged as under a Turkish pasha (Lively and Rees, 1978, p. 120). It is not simply that the poor and their champions might be tempted to commit what Victorian liberals called 'mistakes in political economy'. In seeking to redistribute wealth, democratic governments would inevitably strengthen the powers of the state and erode the freedom of the individual.

This is an argument which finds echoes on the New Right today. Democracies encourage a lack of budgetary restraint and distributive concepts of justice which undermine the unfettered choices of the free market (Hayek, 1960, p. 106). All who cherish freedom should guard against the dangers of the 'unrestricted' will of the majority.

It is true that from the mid-nineteenth century a process of 'redefining' democracy becomes evident. Bryce notes that American politicians are beginning to identify 'plutocracy' (which the ancients classified as oligarchy) with democracy itself (Bryce, 1889, p. 492; see also Dahl, 1985, p. 82), and the pressures of the two world wars persuaded even European liberals that a conceptual adherence to democracy was essential if popular support was to be harnessed to the national cause. By the 1950s, as Arblaster has pointed out (1984, pp. 329–30), American liberal political scientists are using arguments in *defence* of democracy which their liberal predecessors had used against the concept two generations before.

This historical argument certainly throws a sceptical light on the liberal claim to democracy. If liberals themselves concede (or at least conceded in days when political frankness was not an electoral liability) that capitalism is *threatened* by democracy, then it would seem that only those who favour 'equality in rank and fortune' can legitimately call themselves democrats. In today's world this surely means socialists of one hue or another.

DEMOCRACY AND THE PROBLEM OF STATISM

There is however a problem with simply adopting the historical argument in this form. If liberals have traditionally opposed democracy, one of their fears has been that democracy would inflate the powers of the state. This anti-statism has an important bearing on the question of democracy because it is difficult to see how people can be said to govern themselves while living in the shadow of an institution which, as Max Weber reminds us, claims a monopoly of legitimate force in a given territorial area (1964, p. 156).

If liberals have recently appeared to generate confusion and ambiguity over democracy by revising and redefining classical views of the subject, these earlier concepts were not without an ambiguity of their own. The democracy practised in Athens during the fourth and fifth centuries BC is open to an obvious objection. How can it be said that democracy is a system of popular rule when the real majority – the slaves, women and resident aliens – are excluded from the franchise? This is the basis for Schumpter's argument just after the Second World War that democracy has nothing to do with an 'ideal' system of government since the demos must be allowed to define the ranks of the 'people' for themselves (1947, p. 245). There can be nothing inherently 'undemocratic' about excluding Jews, women, blacks or communists. Let the people decide!

This is an important argument because it raises acutely the conceptual problem of yoking democracy to the state. It is true that Greek democrats do appear to have sometimes confused the stateless democracies of tribal times (shrouded in the mists of antiquity) with the slave-owning, statist democracies of the fourth and fifth century BC, but in general the ancients assumed that because democracy is a form of the state, then hierarchical and discriminatory institutions naturally form part of its working.

This is a problem which opponents of democracy have seldom hesitated to exploit. As the New England divine John Cotton asked in the seventeenth century: if everyone governs themselves in a democracy, over whom are they supposed to *govern*? H. G. Wells recalls that when the supreme ruler of the moon was told that governments exist on earth in which 'everyone rules', he immediately called for cooling sprays to be applied to his brows (Cornforth, 1977, p. 244)!

Such extra-terrestrial scepticism would seem well founded, for how is self-government possible when the very existence of the state presupposes a clear cut cleavage between rulers and ruled? Crick might seek to 'defend' politics in the name of conciliation and consensus, but he is obliged to concede the fact that politics presupposes the existence of an institution (that is, the state) with the acknowledged right to use force 'if all else fails' (1982, p. 30).

States arise where communities are too divided to rule themselves. This is a point which preoccupied all the great thinkers of the past from Plato to Marx. There is surely something rather extraordinary (and illogical) about an institution which seeks to promote social harmony and the common good through coercive and hierarchical institutions which of necessity reflect and perpetuate a divided community. Marx called the state 'a theological concept' because he believed that it could only transcend theoretically or 'spiritually' the divisive cleavages of earthly practice (1975, p. 154). His 'theological concept' critically echoes Hobbe's memorable description of the state as a 'Mortal God' (1968, p. 227) and recalls the paradoxical position of Rousseau's Lawgiver.

The problem is this. If democracy is a form of state, then clearly the people 'as a whole' cannot be said to rule. Given the 'monopolistic' and coercive character of all states, it might be argued, as Marxists did in the 1920s and 1930s, that political or statist democracy is itself a kind of dictatorship. An influential British text of the time characterized the early Soviet state as a *democracy* on the grounds that it was democratic for one section of the community and dictatorial for another. 'The small circle of the employers of labour had no voice whatever in the making of the laws to which they were subject' (Sloan, 1937, p. 13). It is the democracy of ancient Greece turned inside out since now the slaves are the masters and the exploiters their servants!

Democracy, in this view, is not really about self-government as such – it is about class rule. It is a form of the state which, as Lenin argues in 1918, 'recognises the subordination of the minority to the majority i.e. an organisation for the systematic use of force by one class against another' (1964, p. 456). The demos is said to be democratically dictating to its 'enemies', but given the existence of the state, the task of confining these 'dictatorial' pressures to a minority is surely an impossible one. After all, the state exercises its monopoly of legitimate force over society as a whole. It is a sovereign body with universal jurisdiction. Majorities acting oppressively towards minorities must also act oppressively towards themselves. The law coerces everyone.

I want to return later to the problem of the socialist state, but here I contend merely that statist definitions, whether ancient or modern, cannot provide a satisfactory analysis of the democratic concept.

A MORE COMPLICATED RELATIONSHIP

Once we introduce the state as a problem for democracy, the opposition between classical liberalism and democracy becomes more complex, for the historical argument invoked earlier cuts two ways: if it points to a tension between liberalism and democracy, it also implies what Crick calls an element of 'harmony' in the relationship (1982, p. 59).

American republicans may have been suspicious about democracy, but they did not oppose it root and branch. They were prepared to concede 'a democratical branch in the constitution' (Hofstadter, 1967, pp. 6 & 14) provided it was checked and balanced by a strong executive and independent supreme court.

The democratic credentials of this republican argument seem unconvincing. After all the United States did not have adult *male* suffrage until the 1840s and even then these political rights did not extend to slaves or indigenous Indians. On the other hand if America (at least for the first part of the nineteenth century) was simply a liberal republic and *not* a democracy, why, for example, did Tocqueville consider the country a veritable laboratory for analysing 'the shape of democracy itself' (1966, p. 17)?

Tocqueville based his argument upon what he saw as a *logic* at work – a social revolution taking place whose progress, he contended, was irresistible and providential. It had begun in America. Soon it would spread to the whole 'Christian world'. 'All have been driven pell-mell along the same road' (1966, p. 8). The logic has an unmistakeably emancipatory thrust: does anyone imagine that democracy, which has destroyed the feudal system and vanquished feudal kings, will fall back before the middle classes and the rich?

Tocqueville is not the only commentator to have seen what he called 'the democratic principle' at work within liberal ideology and institutions. From the seventeenth century onwards liberals were persistently characterized by their conservative opponents as *democrats*. Locke, for example, was accused of wanting to 'poll the whole nation' (Dunn, 1979, p. 4), while King Charles reproached the parliamentarians in the same way that the parliamentarians reproached the radicals. Liberalism encourages servants to become masters: it spawns the anarchistic excesses of democracy! And yet these changes are made at a time when even the radical Levellers did not support the case for universal citizenship.

Charles's critique of the parliamentarians is particularly revealing.

The parliamentarians are 'democrats', he complains, because they confuse a *subject* with a *sovereign*. They fail to see that freedom can only consist in 'having a government' (Dunn, 1979, p. 3). It is a charge which brings us face to face with a remarkable fact: classical liberals may not have considered themselves democrats, but they espoused a creed nevertheless which was even more subversive in its implications than the democratic ideologies of the ancient world.

THE SUBVERSIVE ABSTRACTIONS OF CLASSICAL LIBERALISM

Liberals in the seventeenth and eighteenth century believed that everyone has a natural right to life, liberty and property. Distinctions between master and servant are, even the 'authoritarian' Hobbes tells us, purely conventional: there are few so foolish that would not rather govern themselves than be governed by others (1968, p. 225).

This thesis dramatically explodes the basis of traditional political theory – the belief that the state (with all its divisions and hierarchies) is natural and pre-ordained. It was an argument which alarmed conservatives and sometimes even startled liberals themselves. As late as 1895 D. G. Ritchie could complain that the natural rights doctrine was still capable of mischief as a result of its 'negativity', its critical 'abstractedness' and its rejection of the 'concrete facts of social life and history' (1895, p. 14). By the early nineteenth century Paine and Godwin had already pushed the natural rights theory in the direction of anarchism and social democracy, thus making Tocqueville's point: why stop with feudalism? Natural rights also challenge the social privileges of the middle classes and the rich.

Anarchists and anthropologists have long argued that for many thousands of years humanity governed its affairs without a state. Lacking literate philosophers, however, early tribal societies practised democracy but produced no democratic theory. Liberal ideologists, on the other hand, may have opposed the 'rule of the poor', but they did have a critical attitude to the state, and it is this anti-statism which unleashed a logic of equality alien to both ancient and medieval thought – a theoretical egalitarianism which Tocqueville took as the heart of the democratic principle. The emancipatory thrust of this logic is as dramatic as it is simple. If the state is an artificial and conventional institution, what is to stop people from governing themselves?

Yet the classical liberals were neither anarchists nor egalitarians. The purpose of constructing a state of nature (where individuals were said to live outsidc of society) was to show that inalienable freedoms could only be safeguarded if in the last analysis people *abandoned* a life of anarchy and formed a state. Even Rousseau, who warns us that social contracts are often phoney and repressive, ends up arguing for a 'legitimate state' without which freedom and self-mastery, morality and intelligence cannot really develop (1968, p. 49).

In other words, liberalism suffered from what a youthful David Easton acutely diagnoses as a 'schizoid malady' (1949, p. 18) – an incorrigible tendency to contradict emancipatory principles in social and political practice. Whatever classical liberals said about a natural right to self-government, they were not (and did not pretend to be) democrats. Locke took servants for granted and even constructed an argument to justify slavery. The American republicans expropriated the land of those they were pleased to call 'merciless savages' in the Declaration of Independence, and in South Carolina, for example, human chattels were given as bounty to soldiers who volunteered for the revolutionary cause. It is surprising that royalists should have ridiculed the universalist pretentions of the 'rights of man'?

In *Democracy in America* Tocqueville devotes a scathing chapter to American racial policy towards Indians and blacks – but how did black slavery and Indian expropriation, so integral to the development of nineteenth century America, square with the egalitarian passions of an 'immense and complete democracy' (1966, p. 390)? This is a vital question to tackle if we are to bring the two sides of our historical argument into focus. Liberals appeared to be what they were not. The emancipatory logic of their arguments may have alarmed conservatives but it was a logic accompanied by a whole spectrum of statist and social hierarchies ranging from patriarchy and colonialism to outright slavery.

How is this tantalizing paradox to be explained?

THE EMANCIPATORY LOGIC OF A CONTRADICTORY CAPITALISM

Locke's classic state of nature (which continues to impress New Right libertarians today) takes us to the heart of the problem. People, we are told, live 'naturally' outside of society and yet they clearly have a well-developed sense of their own self-interest. Why was such a bizarre idea plausible to generations of liberal thinkers?

These rational and resolutely abstract individuals are, as Locke makes clear, *exchanging* goods and services and it is these acts of exchange which furnish the key to our riddle. For the exchange process demonstrates how individuals can act together while apparently remaining wholly apart, how they can engage in an activity which instantly mystifies its own social and relational character.

Objects can only exchange, as Marx points out in *Capital*, when each has a value equal to the other. But how can objects which have different physical properties (and have been produced quite differently) have something in common which 'equates' them? The answer: they are the common product of human labour; not of this or that particular kind of labour, but of human labour in the *abstract*. This is a theoretical discovery which is only possible when equality acquires 'the fixity of a popular prejudice' (Marx, 1970, p. 60).

Hence the 'metaphysical subtleties and theological niceties of commodity production' (1970, p. 73). Commodities are real and yet 'abstract', and so are the 'rational individuals' who exchange them. Contracts appear as a relationship between two independent agents each autonomous of the other. Real differences in position and power are concealed. Society and the state themselves emerge as the products of a 'social contract'; of rational exchange; of deliberate consent. It is the logic of the exchange process, of this commodity production which enables us to decode the emancipatory (and yet highly mystifying) logic of classical liberalism.

Already Locke has shown how exchanges in the state of nature (that is, the 'pure' market) lead to the introduction of money and with the existence of money, people 'agree' to 'a disproportionate and unequal possession of the earth' (1924, p. 140). Not only are servants assumed but so is patriarchy. The (representative) relationship between magistrate and subject must be distinguished, Locke insists, from the (presumably despotic) relationship of 'a father over his children, a master over his servant, a husband over his wife and a lord over his slave' (1927, p. 118).

These proliferating hierarchies accord perfectly, as Marx demonstrates, with the logic of commodity production. Accumulating capital and trading in slaves is only possible through conquest and colonialism; servants make themselves available when peasant lands are expropriated. As mercantile yields to industrial capital, wage labour replaces outright slavery. There arises a class of 'free labourers' whose 'labour power' is the miraculous commodity able to generate more value than it itself possesses.

The logic of capitalist production is at the root of the emancipatory logic of classical liberalism. A social realm emerges which is apparently independent of the state, and individuals become seemingly detached from hierarchical identities. Even the proletarians have to be 'emancipated slaves' before they can be exploited. Wealth undreamed of in bygone ages is generated by a 'constant revolutionising of production', by a dynamic which provides the practical basis for theoretical enlightenment. All that is solid melts into air, all that is holy is profaned, and people are compelled to face with sober senses their real conditions of life and their relations with others (Marx and Engels, 1967, p. 83).

The crucial point about this argument is that it is capitalism and capitalism alone which makes the case for 'real' communism as the system which *transcends* it. In precisely the same way liberalism makes the case for democracy. Its emancipatory logic is rooted in (and ideologically reconstructs) the logic of capitalism. In both cases, this logic is fluid and contradictory.

Take the 'metaphysical subtleties and theological niceties' of commodity production as reflected in the capital–labour relationship. It might be supposed that when workers enter into contracts with capitalists, they act as rational individuals whose formal legal rights mask their real lack of social power. Why shouldn't they remain mesmerized by this 'juridical illusion' so that even when they become citizens with a vote, they merely follow what James Mill called the 'advice and example' of the virtuous middle rank? The poor may have political rights, Mill believed, but government would remain 'the business of the rich' (Macpherson, 1977, p. 42). The democratic franchise simply expresses politically the economic hypocrisy of the capital–labour contract. Hence the oft-expressed Marxist verdict: 'bourgeois democracy' is farcical and false!

Crucial to Marx's analysis of capitalism however is the insistence on *contradiction*. When workers sell their labour power they are compelled to move out of the atomistic realm of individualistic exchanges into a social world of production. To survive even as the market vendors of labour power, workers must *combine*, otherwise (given the pressures of capitalist competition to depress wage rates) there is no way they can secure a 'fair price' for the commodity they are selling – that is, their labour power. If propertyless producers are to enjoy their individual rights, they must seek to exercise *collective* power in order to do so. The market itself compels them to invoke what Marx calls 'standards entirely foreign to commodity production' (1970, p. 586).

In other words, equal rights inevitably generate a demand for equal *power*. Legal equality creates pressure for political equality, but political rights alone cannot satisfy the victims of this egalitarian hypocrisy, for 'proletarians' belong to a class whose individuality is not a condition to be protected but a social reality which is yet to be attained. People can only think of themselves as autonomous individuals if they enjoy real power over their lives. Hence we see how political rights become what the Chartists called knife and fork questions. They are valuable as instruments to attain *social* reform.

The logic is contradictory. To remain liberals, those who are the victims rather than beneficiaries of capitalism must become democrats, and since to be a democrat you must address yourself to questions of resources and power, Michael Foot rather than Margaret Thatcher has got it right. Democracy comes into the world tied implicitly to social equality and hence to socialism.

What I have called the emancipatory logic of liberalism is however intimately involved in the process. For the demand for democracy (and thus for socialism) is a product of capitalism. It can only emerge as workers are compelled to turn the weapons of the bourgeoisie (their abstract rights) against this or that aspect of the capitalist system.

Liberalism, to continue with the imagery of the *Manifesto*, creates democracy in precisely the same way as capitalism creates its own grave digger. Its emancipatory logic is self-transcending. The democratic principle may be inherent in the subversive abstractions of the liberal tradition, but it only begins to bite as its egalitarian logic challenges the power of the middle classes and the rich.

DEMOCRATIZING LIBERALISM: ONCE AGAIN THE PROBLEM OF THE STATE

To talk of transcending capitalism is to talk of revolution and this necessarily brings us back to the problem of the state. The *Communist Manifesto* unhesitatingly emphasizes the need for a political strategy to realize communism. The working class must become 'a ruling class' as the first step in 'winning the battle of democracy' (Marx and Engels, 1967, p. 104). Even though Neil Harding has ingeniously argued that Marx turns to a different transitional model in his later analysis of the Paris Commune (1981, pp. 86–7), it is not difficult to show that the Commune with its emphasis on decentralization and popular participation was still regarded by Marx (and not simply by Engels) as a form of the *state*. True, they thought of it as 'a thoroughly expansive political form' (1971, p. 75), but the Marxist classics nowhere deny that it takes a state to get rid of the state – even if the *socialist* state has the historic task of dissolving itself back into society so that, in the *Manifesto*'s words, the public power loses its political character (Marx and Engels, 1967, p. 105).

The problem is how? How is it possible to introduce democracy as genuine self government into a society dominated by hierarchy and underpinned by exploitation? If a revolutionary *state* is necessary to restructure a reactionary order, how does this bring us closer to real freedom? It is for this reason that Macpherson argues that his participatory model of a 'liberal democracy' cannot work in what he calls 'a post-revolutionary situation'. Revolutions provoke counter-revolutions (or the threat of them) and as a consequence democratic control yields to central authority. A new statism supplants the old. This is the fateful lesson of October 1917 (1977, p. 107).

It is a problem which has been anticipated in the Marxist classics. The preference which Marx and Engels have for 'peaceful transitions' over violent ones seems to suggest that the more 'authoritarian' the revolution, the more difficult it is for the post-revolutionary society to usher in popular rule.

There is a further factor to consider. Transcending the state through democracy is naturally tied to the process of transcending capitalism and the market. The relevance of this most classical of Marxist propositions has been made strikingly clear by contemporary upheavals in Eastern Europe, for these upheavals painfully pose the question which refuses to go away: can a socialist society be successfully constructed on the basis of backward rather than advanced capitalism?

It is true that the Marxist classics do not exclude a catalytic role for 'backward' countries in the revolutionary process. Indeed, the very notion of the proletariat as a universal class with radical chains is first formulated in the context of 'autocratic' Germany. It is Germany which also provides the setting for the notion that a delayed 'bourgeois revolution' can unleash the momentum for an immediately-following proletarian one. In 1882 Marx and Engels believed that the revolutionary overthrow of (an even more backward and autocratic) Tsarism will provide 'the signal for proletarian revolution in the West' (1967, p. 56).

But the fact still remains: 'scientific socialism' looks to communism as a product of capitalism – as the 'transcendental' inheritor of its technology, its work discipline and its liberal political culture. Moreover, this is not just capitalism as regionally confined, but capitalism as an international economy embracing the financial and industrial centres of the world. 'We should drop the illusion', a Hungarian has ruefully commented recently, 'that socialism can be built in countries isolated from world capitalism, and that a special "world socialist economic system" can be created' (Aczel, 1989, p. 26).

The construction of socialist societies in backward societies with backward economies has created formidable problems for the process of democratizing and thus transcending (rather than merely negating) liberalism. The more authoritarian the socialist state the more difficult it is to see how the 'battle for democracy' has been decisively won. Workers may constitute the 'ruling class' of the new socialist order but in what sense can it be said that the public power is ceasing to be political when this power remains concentrated and repressive in character?

The new socialist state might be said to be embryonically (or potentially) democratic but as long as it is still dictating to its enemies, is it not vulnerable to all the arguments deployed in the 1950s against the 'totalitarian' practices of 'positive freedom'? The problem is basically this. If people are not doing things for themselves, how can they be said to enjoy freedom and autonomy?

No question has vexed Marxists in the West more than the question of democracy under 'existing socialism'. Take the case of the British communist philosopher who after a lifetime of loyalty to socialist states, comes to wonder (in anguish) as to what counts as progress towards communism. For anyone acquainted with life in the Soviet Union, Maurice Cornforth wrote shortly before his death in 1980, it would seem that 'we are in fact just as near to communism in many respects here in bourgeois England' (1980, p. 213). Cornforth was impressed at the social services and the human values which had, he believed, come to prevail under contemporary capitalism and his argument predates the socialist radicalism of Mikhail Gorbachev and the capitalist radicalism of Margaret Thatcher.

'Bourgeois England' and 'Soviet Russia' have changed significantly since Cornforth commented in despair. On the one hand, Gorbachev has recognized the problem of overcoming a legacy of authoritarian backwardness as no other Soviet leader since Lenin. The banner of glasnost and perestroika has been raised in the name of 'democratization'.

At the same time the Thatcher (counter) revolution has broken with the reformist statism of the New Liberal and labourist tradition. Power must be given back to the people! Of course the 'anti-statism' of the New Right is rhetorical rather than real, but Thatcherism has nevertheless (while concentrating and centralising political power) focused attention as never before upon the state as a barrier to emancipation and democracy. If the notion that British Tories are the pioneers of world revolution is somewhat implausible, can we not credit the New Right with compelling socialists to look again at the radical logic of classical liberalism?

When it comes to 'the real democrats', our preference is clear. We back the socialists against the liberals but with this proviso: 'real democracy' is only defensible as a *post-liberal* phenomenon. It instantly becomes paradoxical and problematic when laced with pre-liberal legacies. This is surely the rational kernel of Cornforth's point. You short-circuit the emancipatory logic of liberalism at your peril! It is also the point which Marx and Engels themselves made in 1845: if proletarians want to assert themselves as *individuals*, they must get rid of the state (1976, p. 46).

REFERENCES

Aczel, G. (1989) 'No Alternative to Democratisation', *World Marxist Review*, 7, pp. 24–8.

Arblaster, A. (1984) *The Rise and Decline of Western Liberalism* (Oxford: Basil Blackwell).

Bryce, J. (1889) *The American Commonwealth*, vol. 2 (London: Macmillan).

Cornforth, M. (1977) *The Open Philosophy and the Open Society*, rev. edn (London: Lawrence and Wishart).

Cornforth, M. (1980) *Communism and Philosophy* (London: Lawrence and Wishart).

Crick, B. (1982) *In Defence of Politics*, 2nd edn (Harmondsworth: Penguin).

Dahl, R. (1985) *A Preface to Economic Democracy* (Cambridge: Polity).

Dunn, J. (1979) *Western Political Theory in the Face of the Future* (London: Cambridge University Press).

Easton, D. (1949) 'Walter Bagehot and Liberal Realism', *American Political Science Review*, 43, pp. 17–37.
Foot, M. (1979) 'Introduction' to *People for the People*, ed. D. Rubenstein (London: Ithaca Press).
Hamilton, A. et al. (1961) *The Federalist Papers* (New York: Basic Books).
Harding, N. (1981) *Lenin's Political Thought*, vol. 2 (London: Macmillan).
Hayek, F. (1960) *The Constitution of Liberty* (London and Henley: Routledge and Kegan Paul).
Hobbes, T. (1968) *Leviathan* (Harmondsworth: Penguin).
Hoffman, J. (1988) *State, Power and Democracy* (Sussex: Wheatsheaf Books).
Hofstadter, R. (1967) *The American Political Tradition* (London: Jonathan Cape).
Lenin, V. I. (1964) *Collected Works*, vol. 25 (Moscow: Progress Publishers).
Lively, J. and Rees, J. (1978) *Utilitarian Logic and Politics* (Oxford: Clarendon Press).
Locke, J. (1927) *Two Treatises of Government* (London: Everyman).
Macpherson, C. B. (1977) *Life and Times of Liberal Democracy* (Oxford, London and New York: Oxford University Press).
Marx, K. (1970) *Capital*, vol. 1 (London: Lawrence and Wishart).
Marx, K. and Engels, F. (1967) *The Communist Manifesto* (Harmondsworth: Penguin).
Marx, K. and Engels, F. (1971) *On the Paris Commune* (Moscow: Progress Publishers).
Marx, K. and Engels, F. (1975) *Collected Works*, vol. 3 (London: Lawrence and Wishart).
Marx, K. and Engels, F. (1976) *Collected Works*, vol. 6 (London: Lawrence and Wishart).
Ritchie, D. G. (1895) *Natural Rights* (New York and London: Macmillan and Swan Sonnenschein).
Rousseau, J. J. (1968). *The Social Contract* (Harmondsworth: Penguin).
Schumpter, J. (1947) *Capitalism, Socialism and Democracy*, 2nd edn (New York and London: Harper).
Sloan, P. (1937) *Soviet Democracy* (London: Victor Gollancz).
Thatcher, M. (1989) cited in 'Thatcher lays claim to torch of freedom', *Independent*, October 14.
Tocqueville, Alexis de (1966) *Democracy in America*, vol 1 (London: Fontana).
Weber, M. (1964) *The Theory of Social and Economic Organisation* (New York and London: Free Press and Collier Macmillan).
Weldon, T. D. (1953) *The Vocabulary of Politics* (Harmondsworth: Penguin).

5 Which Rights of Citizenship?

Michael Rustin

This chapter examines the definitions of rights of citizenship which are currently being advanced by campaigns for radical democracy in Britain, in particular the campaign initiated by Charter 88. The Charter, launched in December 1988, has received a great deal of publicity and support from liberals, radicals and socialists on the left of the political spectrum, and to date (April 1990) has been endorsed by upwards of 17000 signatories, many of them luminaries of the worlds of literature and the other arts, academia, journalism, and other professions including law. The chapter will consider the relationship between the agenda of democratization and extended rights advanced by the Charter, and concerns with issues of social and economic entitlement usually thought of as socialist rather than liberal. It will in this way address the specific concerns of this book on Socialism and Democracy.

CONSTITUTIONAL REFORM AND CHARTER 88

In the past two years or so considerable momentum has developed around campaigns for enhanced civil and political rights in the United Kingdom. Charter 88, which has brought together and given fresh impetus to many of these concerns, calls for a 'new constitutional settlement which would enshrine, by means of a Bill of Rights, such civil liberties as the right to peaceful assembly, to freedom of association, to freedom from discrimination, to freedom from detention without trial, to trial by jury, to privacy and freedom of expression'. This proposed Bill or Rights is largely concerned with the entrenchment of the rights of individual citizens against the arbitrary exercise of the power of the State, though rights to assembly and association also involve the exercise of individual rights in common and for collective purposes.

The Charter identifies a second area of concerns, in proposing that a written constitution should 'subject executive powers and prerogatives, by whomsoever exercised, to the rule of law', should 'ensure the independence of a reformed judiciary', and should provide 'legal remedies of all abuses of power by the state and the officials of central and local government'. The Charter proposes to 'place the executive under the power of a democratically renewed parliament and all agencies of the state under the rule of law'. This set of concerns is largely with the excessive growth of executive power, a recurrent concern of British political life for at least two hundred years, if not since Magna Carta.

The third category of rights identified by Charter 88 concerns what we think of as the exercise of positive political citizenship, through forms of electoral and territorial representation, fair or otherwise. To enforce these rights, Charter 88 calls for the 'guarantee of an equitable distribution of power between local, regional and national government', for the 'reform of the upper house to establish a democratic, non-hereditary second chamber', and for 'a fair electoral system of proportional representation'.

Charter 88 has not been by any means the only grouping recently concerned with these various issues – electoral reform has been actively supported by the SLD, the Social Democrats, and by the Labour Campaign for Electoral Reform. The 'national question', only faintly gestured to in the Charter, has been made a major issue by the Scots, and in a different and more tragic way by the twenty years of armed conflict in Northern Ireland. The Campaign for Press Freedom has fought for freedom of information, and even more important to the defence of these rights have been the numbers of brave individuals, journalists, editors, broadcasters, and others who have been willing to risk or suffer imprisonment for their calling or for what they have seen as the public good. There is also the vital work, over a long period, of organizations such as the NCCL and Amnesty International in resisting abuses of individual rights. Nevertheless, the Charter is the first successful attempt for a long period to bring all these concerns together in one unified campaign, and it can therefore be taken as the basis for reflection on what should be included or excluded in the idea of 'rights of citizenship'.

THE STRANGE OMISSION OF SOCIAL AND ECONOMIC RIGHTS

What is striking about Charter 88's definition of rights is its very traditional, if not archaic, limitation and exclusiveness. The rights it proclaims, to individual freedom under the law, to the subordination of government to the rule of law, and to democratic forms of representation, pre-date the agendas of the collectivistic liberalism of the early twentieth century, never mind the social democracy of its middle years, which each attempted in their different ways to demonstrate that social and economic rights were as indispensable as political and civil rights to the exercise of citizenship. T. H. Marshall (1950), in his famous essay *Citizenship and Social Class*, set out a three-stage historical model of the development of citizenship in Britain, locating the rise of civil, political, and social citizenship as achievements of the eighteenth, nineteenth, and twentieth century respectively, though universal suffrage was not of course fully won in Britain until 1928.[1] These social rights, usually often thought of as the basis of the welfare state, include rights to a minimum income in conditions of illness, unemployment or old age, to free education, to improved housing, and to health care. We should add to this list Beveridge's idea of a right to work, made largely effective for several decades after the Second World War by full-employment policies. Indeed, the Beveridge Report, with its identification of the 'Giant Evils' – Want, Disease, Ignorance, Squalor and Idleness – that needed to be remedied, was the most influential public statement of this social rights agenda.

The emergence of these social rights on to the political agenda reflected also the rise of mass democracy and the participation of working class populations, and also women (greatly influencing the preoccupations of the welfare state[2]), in political life. The decision of those now campaigning for rights of citizenship to exclude these conceptions seems to mark out these campaigns as those of a narrower social stratum than those committed to these broader twentieth century definitions. What is included and excluded by Charter 88's definition of rights seems to justify the view of this movement's critics that it is essentially middle class in its concerns. For those already actively involved in political participation (by no means a representative cross-section of the population, in either class, gender or ethnic terms), or engaged by vocation in the communication of information and ideas, the Charter's aims may seem central. But for those worried more about the social infrastructure of their lives, about ensuring the conditions which might provide time, skill, confidence, and material resources to spare for the active exercise of political citizenship, the Charter might seem to have rather less to offer.

Even in the sphere of civil and political rights, incidentally, the Charter hasn't much to say about those inequities and injustices attributable to ethnicity and gender. There is no claim, even in the most general terms, that representation should more fairly reflect than it now does the gender and ethnic make-up of the population, nor is there critical mention of social practices which discriminate by ethnicity or gender. The Charter refers to the 'arbitrary diktat of Westminster and Whitehall', but in practice its own preoccupations are closer to those who frequent these locations than to the daily worries of the inhabitants of Brixton, Barking, or Basildon. This campaign for popular democracy has a remarkably élitist flavour.

Those responsible for framing the Charter are not, of course, indifferent to social issues. Most of them would acknowledge connections between social rights and entitlements, and the equal exercise of political liberties. A judgement was made, however, that it is the unrestrained power of the State which at this point is the main threat to liberties of all kinds. The electoral system, and the overwhelming power which the British constitution has conferred on the Thatcher Governments (none of which has won a majority of popular votes) are held responsible in the last resort for all the other invasions of rights – in the spheres of welfare, trade unions, civil liberties and so on – which have been perpetrated since 1979. In the background of all this is a historical theory which argues that the British State, unlike other contemporary States born out of revolution or its virtual equivalent imposed after military defeats, was never properly subjected to a democratic, pluralist, or liberal renovation, still less revolution. It merely grafted majority party rule on top of many features of monarchical and aristocratic government, in a period when the scope of power exercised by the State (over the economy, welfare, military mobilization, communications, and so on) was vastly increasing. One version of this argument, not without its background influence in Charter 88 circles, equates this relative failure of democratization with the non-achievement of a British 'bourgeois revolution'. This however involves a rather special reading of 'bourgeois revolution', which equates 'bourgeois' with 'democratic'. Historically, the connection with capitalism and the triumph of the bourgeoisie, and democracy has not always been so close. Furthermore, if Thatcherism, with its 'authoritarian populist' conception of the role of the State, isn't some kind of attempted 'bourgeois revolution', what is it?[3]

These imputed links, between constitutional arrangements and social class hegemony, have enabled the instigators of the Charter to draw some second-order or indirect connections between their liberal definition of rights, and the broader social rights objects which in practice they mostly share. *If* Charter 88's proposals were to be implemented, continuation of 'ideological' governments of the Thatcherite kind would seem to become unlikely. Many of those who supported the launch of the Charter saw it as serving to link Labour and SLD in a *de facto* alliance against the Thatcher Governments. (The Charter was initiated before the collapse of electoral support for the SLD. The SLD and Social Democrat interest in this project is obvious – without such a political alliance, the electoral reforms on which their long-term prospects depend is virtually out of the question.) Socialist interest in electoral reform in particular comes from some who take a long view of Labour's declining electoral prospects, to which they see electoral reform as a solution; and from dissidents on the left who would like to see a more open and competitive context for oppositional politics than the Labour Party now provides. Those influenced by the thesis of the failed British bourgeois revolution also see Labourism as having been fatally limited by this and by its self-chosen role as constitutional opposition and alternative government-in-waiting. These critics have a more Gramscian concept of political change, and of the role of the intelligentsia within it. The prominent role of intellectuals within the Charter follows from this too.

However, these putative connections, between constitutional reforms and wider social changes which might enhance social and economic rights, are for the long run, and in any case have been given neither public nor private emphasis in Charter 88 debates. Despite the degree of convergence between collectivist liberal and democratic socialist positions on these questions, social rights issues have been avoided, perhaps because it was feared that they would divide the fragile coalition at the core of the Charter. This anxiety may also have been in part based on an illusory hope that this 'non-party' campaign might stretch all the way over the political spectrum, to include Conservatives too. But in practice, few Conservatives have signed the Charter.

The confinement of the Charter's agenda to issues which can be defined broadly as liberal has probably limited its range of appeal.

Clearly journalists and writers for whom free expression is a direct and even material condition of life care deeply about these questions, as may the politically sophisticated who can see that these other issues are joined to constitutional questions in a probable chain of cause and effect. Electoral reform in particular gains support, as a likely means to many other political changes. But excepting the minority highly conscious of such linkages, the Charter appears to have nothing to say about deficits of economic or social rights, whether these arise from considerations of gender, race, or class. If the main concern of most people is with the tangible conditions and opportunities of their lives, then a programme like Charter 88's may well leave most citizens unmoved, and perhaps thereby doom itself to the fate of lost liberal causes.

By contrast, in Eastern Europe (it was from the Czechoslovak Charter 77 that Charter 88 took its name) the connections between form of government and economic well-being were always obvious. There never *would* be anything to buy in the shops, and the nomenklatura would always monopolize whatever privileges there were, so long as autocratic political systems remained intact. Here, however, there are many things in the shops, incomes (for a large majority) to buy them with, schools and hospitals (still) to go to. The *extrinsic* reasons for arguing for constitutional reforms are much less pressing than they are (or were) in the East. This different order of connection between the economic and social spheres on the one hand, and the constitutional and political spheres on the other, of Communist and liberal capitalist societies (connections which are almost defining properties of these social orders [Giddens, 1972]) goes a long way to explain the difference of appeal of constitutional reform movements within them.

INDIVIDUAL RIGHTS VERSUS THE WELFARE STATE: THE THATCHERITE PROGRAMME

It is probably more than tactical considerations which explain the reluctance of the constitutional reform campaign to involve itself with this wider agenda of social and economic rights. Such rights have characteristically required the exercise of the coersive powers of government to tax, regulate, and redistribute. The institutions through which such entitlements have been implemented have been, in Britain, typically statist and bureaucratic. Whilst social rights of citizenship – to receive income support, education, health, for example – have been vastly extended even in the post-Second World War period, the conception of citizenship implied in the major forms of provision of welfare has been a passive, not an active one. There is a singular contrast between the power which the State routinely disposes in its treatment of the citizen – taxing them, regulating their economic activity, recording and storing any number of facts about them, removing children from their parents' care where their protection demands it, compulsorily purchasing their property in the public interest, and where need arises conscripting them into the armed services and requiring the sacrifice of their lives – and the rights of citizens in respect of the services the State administers. The State is strong, the citizen weak. The State does, it is true, provide many goods and services to its citizens – income support, grants, subsidies, school and college places, medical treatment and hospital beds. But citizens have scant means to enforce their entitlements to these benefits, or to insist that they should be of a given standard. Even with the most tangible and comparable kinds of benefit – those provided as cash by social security departments – the relation between State and claimants is a notoriously inequitable one. A *de facto* status of diminished citizenship – a kind of informal pauper role – often describes the relation between State servants and claimants better than the formal relationship of citizens receiving entitlements due to them. In the case of services in kind – education, health, local authority services – difficulties in enforcing due standards of provision, or in obtaining redress where services are found wanting, are of a different kind. Providers of services are often in a position of power over their clients, and complaint – about the treatment of a pupil, a patient, or house repairs – may be met by indifference and evasion, or even by covert reprisal, usually without the citizen being able to do much about it.

The post-Beveridge welfare state did at least assume that rights of citizenship were unconnected with the ownership of property. Its assumption was that individuals would pay through taxation as they could afford, and receive in income support and services what they needed up to a defined minimum standard. The community charge or poll tax now calls these assumptions in question in a regressive way. The main justification of the poll tax is that all those who are beneficiaries of local services should contribute to them through local taxation. The representative system is distorted, according to advocates of the poll tax, if a significant proportion of voters are not taxed.

The immediate remedy to this disconnection between the right to vote and the obligation to pay was to make every citizen pay. But of course rebates and exemptions were unavoidable. Once political citizenship and fiscal obligation become re-connected in this way, it would be as logical to restrict rights of political citizenship as it is to generalize obligations to contribute. (However, this might be even more unpopular than the poll tax itself.) This would merely reconstitute the links between property-ownership and voting rights on which the British democratic system was based for centuries.

The purported 'democratic' remedy for the failings of public provision, namely political action, is immensely costly of time and effort, and incidentally discriminates against those who are most likely to seek such remedy through the time and resources it demands. A fact which contributes to this situation is that the political, representative arm of the public system – that whose principal task is two-way communication between government and people – is grossly under-resourced, by a kind of tacit design: part-time councillors without professional assistance for their constituency roles. Members of Parliament with exiguous resources to discharge their many functions – these people cannot provide very wide channels of redress, even though they may spend much of their working time in trying to do so.

It is because of the apparent powerlessness of the citizen in the face of these providers of public goods that the Thatcherites have been able to claim that in their reforms of the welfare state they are seeking to enhance, not reduce, individual freedom. It is a paradox that these exceptionally forceful governments, which have had no reluctance to exercise all the formidable powers available to them, should nevertheless have been able to present themselves as enemies of the power of the State. They have proclaimed the desire to emancipate the citizen from subordination to monopolistic State agencies. They have chosen various methods of doing this. One is the substitution of private for public provision where this is feasible, giving subsidies to new owners where necessary, as with council house sales and private pension schemes. A second method has been to encourage the substitution of 'social market' relations, in the spheres of education and health, for the definitions of public service and entitlement which formerly prevailed in these sectors. Increased choice by 'consumers' of services still provided mainly without charge is meant to force suppliers (medical practices, schools) to become more responsive to individual consumer needs.

A third method of changing the relation of citizen and State in these spheres has been to restrict the powers of elected local government, or of larger nominated health authorities, and instead confer more powers on local providing agencies (for example, schools, colleges, hospitals) or their managers or governing bodies. The 'contracting-out' of services within these welfare sectors, and the encouragement of market principles in relations between providers, also has the effect of transforming 'public service' values and procedures into more competitive, finance-driven, and ultimately individualistic methods of organisation.

These charges to the welfare system, now embodied in a whole series of recent Acts of Parliament and White and Green Papers which affect education, health, and social services (Great Britain 1988, 1989a, 1989b, 1990), represent the second and more active stage of Thatcherite reorganization of these services, after a long period in which feasible reforms (privatization, vouchers, wholesale dismantling) were still being invented and canvassed in the context of bitter wars of attrition, especially with the public sector unions. The 'social market' philosophy embodied in these changes is likely to have lasting effects on the whole welfare system. One reason for this is that these changes open up services to a greater measure of differentiation by income and status, which is consonant with generally greater inequality in British society. The greater the social and economic polarization, the greater the difficulties of maintaining universal services as a means of integrating society, and maintaining an idea of common citizenship. A second reason is that these changes do provide one form of incentive to improve efficiency and responsiveness to demand, in organizations so large and remote from their clients that this did not always readily occur. A third and less noticed reason is that these transformations of the public sector offer new opportunities to public sector managers to take advantage of opportunities, both organisational and personal, provided by competitive social markets. These reforms are likely to have seductive attractions for capable members of the public sector service class, which the more negative first phase of Thatcherism did not have.

These changes have their similarities of purpose and no doubt effects with the marketizing reforms being pursued at the present time in Eastern Europe, as Mrs Thatcher is aware. Such are the difficulties of operating large-scale 'command economies' that even many socialists have endorsed the idea of 'market socialism' as a more promising model of organization (Nove, 1983; Le Grand and

Estrin, 1989; Miller, 1989). Market socialists have argued that the enfranchisement, through redistribution of income or the allocation of 'voucher' entitlements to specific kinds of services, of citizens as 'welfare consumers' is likely to provide both better and more equal standards of provision than the previous bureaucratic/professional systems of welfare.

Another method of reducing the powerlessness of citizens in relation to the providers of public services would be to strengthen the direct elective control of service organisations. Compulsory provision for trade union ballots and elections have followed this route in relation to union power, but this model is less attractive to the Government in regard to the State's own activities. Although the power of elected school governors has been enlarged, *vis-à-vis* those of elected local councils and party nominees, in general the philosophy of government has favoured business principles, and not elective ones, in the composition of governing bodies and their legitimation. I shall go on to argue that there are serious difficulties in the way of increasing the accountability and responsiveness of services by making their organization more elective, desirable as this might be on general grounds.

It seems likely that the avoidance by the constitutional radicals of Charter 88 of the whole field of issues connected with social and economic rights is linked to the problems of adequately defining 'individual rights' in these fields. In this sphere, both the Government and its opponents claim to be defending the rights of the citizen, the former by giving them power to choose, free from the control of monopoly State service-providers, and the latter by defending a still-resonant though now vague idea of universal social entitlement.

The problem for the radical defenders of 'rights' is that the welfare state has on the whole seemed to confer benefits, not 'rights'. It has done so through the machinery of the same hierarchical and passivity-inducing State that Charter 88 seeks to transform in the civil and political sphere. It is not surprising, in these circumstances, that it has seemed simpler for constitutional reformers not to muddy the waters with these problems, and instead leave them entirely aside. The danger is that whilst constitutional radicals make headway with their agenda of civil and political rights, they leave the other agenda, of social and economic rights, in the hands of the Thatcherites. It might even be said that two kinds of individualism – with a left and right inflection – are in practice proceeding on parallel paths.

Some socialists fear that the goals of enhanced citizenship enshrined in the Charter might be antithetical to the collectivistic and egalitarian aims to which they are committed. There are many self-seeking if short-sighted reasons for the Labour Party to remain committed to the present constitutional system, and in particular its electoral arrangements. But the idea that a majoritarian elective system should be used to support egalitarian social goals need be neither self-seeking nor absurd. There is also some plausibility in the idea that the main power resource available to subordinate classes is the power of the State, and that its deployment is often desirable. Would limiting the power of majority governments always be such an unqualified good, given the different aims such governments might in future have? Should one welcome an electoral system that might, for example, make it impossible ever to abolish private education in Britain, because of the constraint it would impose on any single-party government which happened to have less than 50 per cent of the vote?

One doesn't have to be an advocate of a majoritarian absolutism of the left to see that these are real questions. Those concerned most with issues of social and economic well-being may have good reason to worry about the relationship of constitutional reform issues to their concerns. It seems to me vital that constitutional reformers should address these questions, and to explore whether they might have something to say about them from their own principles of enhanced, equal, and active citizenship. Rights of citizenship without a social and economic basis are unlikely to have much substance.

A 'RIGHTS' APPROACH TO WELFARE

The agenda of rights is structured at present in two ways. On the one hand, distinctions can be made between civil, political, and social rights, on the lines set out many years ago by T. H. Marshall. As we have seen, Charter 88 has confined its attention to the first two. A second distinction can be made between alternative means of implementing social and economic rights. The main distinction here is between entitlements pursued through market exchange, regulated by law and convention to a greater or lesser degree, and entitlements provided through elective political processes, in the domains of policy-formation, legislation, and administrative implementation. Marshall, and following him Barbalet (1988), point out that the original achievement of civil rights for individuals was closely linked to the emergence of free market exchange, rights of disposal of property displacing the obligations and rights of inherited status. Roughly speaking, the former (market) system confers more freedom (both as choice and control over what is consumed) but produces less equality. The second system may aim at greater equality or provision in accordance with need, but usually offers rather less choice or control by citizens. The 'social market' approach of recent welfare reforms is designed in part as a compromise between these systems, aiming to combine features of each.

The proposal I want to make is for the enhancement of citizens' power over public services in a rather different mode from that of an increased power of 'exit' (Hirschman, 1970) or individual consumer choice. Hitherto, those concerned with the place of democracy in the economic and political spheres have tended to concentrate on the legislative process, on how 'rights' are brought into being, rather than on the ways in which services and goods are provided, and on the control citizens are given over them. The mobilization of political support, the formation of policy, and the activity of making policies into law, have dominated radical politics. Implementation has been left, mostly, to the professionals and bureaucrats. So if the children's school is no good, the council house does not get repaired, the rubbish does not get collected, the psychiatric patient is not treated, the ageing relative is left inadequately tended in a home, there is usually rather little the average citizen can do about it. Whereas, of course, if the citizens' obligations to the State are not met, and the rates or community charge bill not paid, the authorities will be quick enough off the mark with their summonses and bailiffs.

An alternative approach is to give more attention to the sphere of implementation and delivery of services, that is to the interfaces between providers and 'consumers' of such services. This may be thought of in terms of enhancements of the rights of individuals *vis-à-vis* service providers, and the maintenance of standards of services as these affect their consumers or clients in general. What is being sought here is an approach which focuses neither on the *production* of services, nor on their modes of *consumption*, but rather on their *monitoring and regulation*.

Remedies through the production side of things have argued for different patterns of organization (more decentralized, managerial, marketized, or worker-controlled institutions). Solutions based on consumer power have proposed enhanced choice, through mechanisms such as vouchers, improved flows of information, representation on governing bodies (for example, of schools) and the establishment of bodies representing consumer interests, such as Community Health Councils.[4] The development of consumer information and protection services on a subscription basis, such as those of the Consumers' Association and its offshoots, have been important in this sphere, providing a mutually-provided service to large numbers of individuals. This 'consumers movement' has also been able to bring pressure to bear on governments on standards and so on. These services have enjoyed some limited but important State backing – even the multiple readership provided to *Which* through public libraries represents a public subsidy to consumer powers, just as Law Centres and Citizens Advice Bureaux provide support for citizens in defending their civil and social rights.

The 'third way' proposed here concentrates, however, not on 'producer democracy' or 'consumer self-help', but at the individual level on rights of redress through quasi-judicial procedures, and at the collective level on extended functions of inspection and monitoring of public services. These are seen as a means of enhancing the rights of citizens and of improving the standards of goods and services that are provided for them.

The purpose is to find ways of improving standards of service and well-being which are based on normative and deliberative means and which thus strengthen the ethical and public-spirited basis of public life. This is in contrast to majoritarian 'strategies of equality' of the left, which too often turn a blind eye to their dependence on coercive means, and thus to their vulnerability to liberal criticism and popular resentment. And it is in contrast also to the assumptions of the market reformers of the right, in their private or social variants, for whom the only reliable motivating force is the self-interest of individuals, whether in the role of providers or consumers.

One of the pressing tasks with which this argument is concerned is to find a persuasive conception of citizenship alternative to the definition of the 'citizen as consumer' (Bauman, 1988), which is fast taking over political and cultural life in Britain in the space left by the decay of an earlier ethos of public service.

RESULTS OF INDIVIDUAL REDRESS

Advocates of social rights of citizenship such as Marshall have long acknowledged the difficulties in defining 'social' rights in terms which render them enforceable at law. Barbalet (1988) argues that social and economic rights differ altogether from civil and political rights in being substantive rather than formal, relative rather than absolute. A citizen either does or does not have the right to vote. He either enjoys or does not enjoy rights to freedom of association, or free access to information. Thus legal procedures can be used to define such rights, and to defend them where necessary. Charter 88 is only seeking to reinforce these existing conceptions and entitlements when it aims to have such civil rights incorporated in a written constitution, where they will not be so readily over-ridden by executive power, or the disciplined vote of a Parliamentary majority.

It is surely obvious, however, that many of these 'civil' rights are themselves subject to continuing re-interpretation, with which the courts have to concern themselves. For example, there are the rights citizens should enjoy against the police, and how far particular categories of citizens are liable to find these infringed; or the definition of what should count as an abuse of a woman's or child's rights to be protected from physical or emotional mistreatment within a family; or the degree to which the public should have access to information concerning the activities of the State – these are all instances of highly-contested and variable definitions of rights, by no means clearly distinguishable from a quite other category of 'substantive' social entitlements. In so far as such definitions of civil rights are subject to redefinition as social expectations and norms change, so they seem to acquire a 'substantive' and 'relative' character, similar to those of more obviously 'social' entitlements.

In fact, some entitlements belonging in Marshall's twentieth century sphere of 'social rights' are by their nature better adapted to precise legal definition and enforcement than certain rights which in conceptual terms belong in the civil sphere. Economic entitlements to income support, for example, can or could be as precisely calibrated as liability to taxation. The problem of enforcing justice in this sphere is not a difficulty of definition, but on the contrary the inequity of access of members of different social classes to the law (since, among other reasons, legal services can be purchased and those without the means to pay for them are at some disadvantage), and also because the State often prefers to deal with the poor on a basis of diminished citizenship and semi-pauperization, leaving to the discretion of officials 'benefits' which should mostly be defined as 'entitlements'.

To some degree the apparent increase in actions for negligence against the National Health Service reflect the rise of a climate of material self-interest which it is no part of this argument to support. Nevertheless, the success of such actions does indicate that it is possible to make juridical judgements about failures of care which depend on a reference to current professional standards. Frequently, those complaining of inadequacies of care say that their main concern is not with financial compensation (the idea of monetary compensation for such loss seems sometimes badly to confuse different modes of well-being). Rather they say their main concern is to establish responsibility, and above all to find out the truth. The truth is a public not a private good, and people's motivations here are often altruistic and reparative, that is, to ensure that 'if possible, this never happens again'. It would be to the public good if State institutions were more and not less exposed to such redress by individuals whom they may inadvertently injure or neglect. But while individuals should be liable to compensation for material hardship and loss arising from such neglect, the object of such procedures should be to define and maintain public standards, not encourage the pursuit of private gain. The attachment of monetary values to deprivations (for example, emotional losses) which are inherently not monetary in nature, is an instance of a confusion of 'spheres of justice' which is now contributing significantly to the decay of an ethical public domain.

There are many spheres in which the law has in recent years sought to protect citizens from injustice and harm of various sorts. Legislation concerned with health and safety in the workplace, with employment protection against unfair dismissal, with discrimination on grounds of race, with equal opportunities in regard to gender, with the protection of children from injury and abuse, with the protection of the environment (which is to say of communities' and individuals' legitimate interests in its quality) are some instances. Most if not all of these fields of citizens' protection are concerned with the avoidance of harm, rather than the promotion of good by means of public provision. Nevertheless, the definitions of harm which are enforced by these judicial processes are relative to changing social norms, and to that extent define entitlements of a 'substantive' kind.

The question is whether it would be possible and desirable to make entitlements to adequate standards of public provision or service, by schools, medical practices, or social service departments, enforceable by individuals by means of quasi-judicial processes, in some more positive manner. Could not State agencies become more accountable for what they do or do not provide, by means other than subjecting them to the competition of other service-providers in a market or quasi-market? Could not a strengthened individual 'voice' be provided to users of services, by making complaint more feasible, both for individuals' benefit and for the improvement of services in general? Ombudsman procedures are probably the most widely-used (for example in Sweden) and effective means of meeting this objective. State agencies and their servants prefer not to be inspected, challenged, or held accountable for their failings, but this is no reason why they should not be.

The proposal is that social and economic entitlements to adequate standards of provision should be defined in such ways that it becomes possible to seek redress when they fail to be met. Clearly, this must be a matter of acceptable minimum standards, subject to norms and reasonable expectations prevailing at the time. I have argued elsewhere (Rustin, 1985, 1988) that a right to work is one such entitlement which could and should be enforceable, with the State accepting the role of employer of last-resort, instead of merely as now the role of last-resort guarantor of minimum income.

In many polytechnics and universities procedures have been introduced since the disturbances of the 1960s which entitle students to seek redress if the outcome of their studies, as eventuate in their assessments, has been adversely affected by the negligence of teachers or failures of proper procedures. This system probably serves on the whole to constrain academics to behave in a more consistent and responsible manner towards their students than they otherwise might. If a course is not provided in a way consistent with the prospectus, or if examinations or assessments are not properly set, judgements made of a student's work are vulnerable to challenge. Challenges, in my experience, are relatively few, and are often settled by informal procedures before appeals committees are convened. It is the existence of the right of appeal that makes the difference, making it more difficult to allow injustices or inadequacies to pass, and requiring problems to be thought about objectively (in anticipation of a judicial process) when complaints are made. Whilst academic institutions are especially devoted to deliberative methods, and probably have more resources than most to devote to them, this model may have relevance to other institutions too.

The goal of making economic and social rights more enforceable against the State where this is necessary is consistent with the idea of enhanced citizenship. But it seeks to relate the idea of citizenship more closely to the spheres of material and social well-being than Charter 88's existing agenda now does.

THE INSPECTION AND MONITORING OF PUBLIC SERVICES

The argument above is concerned with enforceable individual rights to standards of service. More important than this, however, may be to develop improved means by which standards can be enforced generally and collectively. Such procedures have a long and distinguished history in British public life. The inspection of factories, of public health, and of education are functions which date back to the nineteenth century (Corrigan and Sayer, 1985). These forms of inquiry and regulation were the first major means by which government became involved in the improvement of standards of well-being, and at that stage were more important than its role in the direct provision of public services. The role of the HMI in the sphere of education, of the Health and Safety Inspectorate, of the Social Services Inspectorate, and of bodies set up to deal with specific fields of discrimination, such as the Community Relations Commission, continue to be important in the regulation of the behaviour of both public and private agencies in their dealings with citizens, though less so than many corresponding regulatory agencies in the United States.

To these statutory institutions we can add the many ad hoc inquiries that are set up to investigate particular abuses, but which are expected also to report on matters of broader public significance arising from them. Inquiries into major accidents such as the Kings Cross or the Ostend Ferry disasters, into circumstances leading to the deaths of children from abuse, or into events such as those concerning child abuse in Cleveland in 1987, are recent examples of such investigations. The present Government has shown an inclination to strengthen such inspectorial functions as these affect *some* public services, for example by imposing a system of Medical Audit in its National Health Service reforms, or less directly in its proposals for national assessments in schools. But in other spheres, for example those concerned with the regulation of private businesses, and in regard to the practice of central State administration, it has tended to go in the other direction and restrict public scrutiny, for example making no concessions, in regard to State activities, to the general principle of freedom of information.

Whilst these various inspectorial functions are important, they do not do much to qualify the generally passive conception of citizenship typical of British government and society. Inspectors are usually experts, following the example of Matthew Arnold as enlightened representatives of the highest traditions of public service, examining *de haut en bas* and then reporting and advising on the work of more humble practitioners of the relevant callings. Or they are judges, trained at balancing and sifting evidence, and at making judicial assessments. The development of more scientific measures, making use of data bases, assessments of comparative performance, and especially today measures of cost-effectiveness, supplements the traditional humanist conception of experienced professional judgement with the resources of social science.

What is lacking in all this is much idea that either the day-to-day practitioner in a public service field, or its ordinary users, will have much to contribute to the task of maintaining standards – except, that is, as witnesses or defendants or complainants when anything goes badly wrong. The citizens is as much a passive citizen in regard to the monitoring of what is done for him or her as in the process of deciding how it should be done. The effect of this inveterately hierarchical construction of public roles is that monitoring, inspection and assessment of services are functions performed from outside and above the services themselves, and have a correspondingly restricted impact on the thinking of the service-providers. The HMI's report is typically made to the head teacher, and it is for him or her to communicate its contents, and make its recommendations effective, among all the teachers and support-workers in the school.

The thinking behind this methodology of the HMI is no doubt that any more direct and 'horizontally oriented' mode of communication might undermine authority within a school or institution, and thus might make matters worse rather than better. But to give such priority to a commitment to 'vertical' or hierarchical structures of organization and communication reveals a traditionalist and narrow vision of how organizations might best function, especially in the diffuse spheres of 'people related' work such as that of health, education, and social services. In forms of work where a high degree of autonomy is necessary to the task (such as teaching, medicine, or social work), professional consensus and commitment is vital to achieving good results. Only if organizational goals are widely supported is a high level of performance likely to result. The problem of improving standards is one of motivation and understanding diffused throughout an institution, not merely of conveying instructions through a factory-like system of line-management. Indeed the imposition of mistaken models of industrial management, with accompanying widening of income and status differentials between the grades of what was formerly seen as an integrated professional workforce, is one of the most misguided consequences of the present Government's public sector reorganizations, all the more so since the models imposed are often becoming obsolete in the private sector (or in its more modern sectors) at the very moment when they are being imposed on the public.

A different model of the inspection and monitoring of public services can be conceived. This would be based on the idea of professional peer review, and of user-voice, and would deploy expert advisers (the traditional 'inspector') and objective performance data (statistical or otherwise) merely as resources in a broader deliberative process. One could envisage such reviews of service-provision taking place on a triennial or six-yearly basis, perhaps with greater levels of formality and external involvement at the longer intervals. Such review procedures might be organized around consideration of a development plan for an institution, which would include a review of its work over the previous period, but would also make use of field-inspections of work, objective data, expert reports, and so on. They would take the form of deliberative inquiry and discussion, over a period of a day or days depending on the size and complexity of the institution. Institutions that might be subject to such procedures include many departments and divisions of local authority services (a school, a children's home, a social services department) or other agencies, such as institutions managed by a health authority or indeed a police division. The smaller the institution, and the clearer its task and organizational boundary, the simpler the procedures for reviewing its work.

The participants in such reviews would include professional advisers and inspectors, experienced professionals from similar agencies elsewhere, representatives of organizations of clients or users, and ordinary citizens chosen by nomination or application or by lot, on the model of the jury service. On the other side would sit members of the organization being reviewed, led by their senior staff, but nevertheless encouraged to participate freely as having voices of their own. The aim of such a process is to encourage deliberation and reflection among all those taking part, so that institutional practices are subjected to friendly but critical examination in a setting which commands serious attention from those participating in it. The *deliberative* and educative functions of democracy, much recommended by John Stuart Mill, are singularly neglected in its everyday practice, and this procedure for reviewing services of which individuals have local and personal experience (whether as users or providers) would help to redress this lack. The importance of the participation of members of similar institutions elsewhere is to encourage the transfer of professional knowledge, especially of good practices, from one institution to another. This is something which is hard to accomplish in spheres of activity which cannot readily be regulated by the market, or by one-dimensional bottom-line criteria of profit and loss. This is inevitably going to be the case in the provision of welfare, where both the diffuseness of goals, and the difficulty of making user-judgements about the relative quality of services, make qualitative and multi-dimensional assessment essential.[5]

Similar procedures to those proposed above could be employed in the accreditation of private or not-for-profit (voluntary sector) institutions to perform welfare tasks on the 'contracting' basis now widely supported by the Government in the field of social and other local government services. This would produce a higher measure of public accountability than is likely to arise merely from entrusting the tasks of contracting-out services to the directors of local government departments.

The model described above of course has a major precedent in the work of the Central Council for National Academic Awards (CNAA) in the development of (mainly) degree level higher education in the polytechnics and colleges of higher education in the past twenty years. CNAA's method has been one of peer review: it has required institutions and course providers to define and justify their own preferred means of achieving national standards in their relevant teaching fields, rather than following an externally prescribed model. Its method of validation (and lately accreditation), through a method of dialogue based on prior documentation, has required institutions to operate in a relatively collegial mode, since representations rarely succeed without a high level of consensus on goals and means being revealed in discussion. Some limited access of students to this review procedure has been another valuable fail-safe device. This method has enabled a large increase in the numbers and proportions of students in higher education to take place, and of the number of major institutions involved in its provision, with little sacrifice of academic standards and a considerable gain in diversity. It has been a major institutional innovation in British public policy, and now that its role is (regrettably) diminishing as polytechnics are granted greater institutional autonomy, it is time that its positive lessons are applied to other settings where they would be relevant.

It will be argued that institutions of higher education are special cases, adapted to the exercise of a kind of 'deliberative citizenship' which would not be feasible for other institutions such as primary schools, social security benefit offices, or local authority housing departments. This argument probably conceals a latent assumption that consultative or democratic procedures are for the gentlemanly or highly-educated only. If we believe in citizenship, what could be more essential than that individuals should have some direct say, either in person of through a representative process, in the governance of the institutions that most directly affect their well-being?

This model of deliberative review makes use, in relation to practical settings, of ideas and principles developed usually in more abstract terms by Jurgen Habermas (McCarthy, 1978; Pusey, 1987). The idea of interactive reflection on ongoing social practices, in conditions where all categories of member and user are represented and entitled to participate, seeks to embody in real terms the ideal of 'undistorted communication' and free communicative interaction. This conception imagines democracy as a process of open and free dialogue about the ends and means of social action in institutions. Even if in day-to-day respects organizations go on (perhaps inevitably) being imperatively coordinated through more-or-less hierarchical chains of command, a requirement of periodic open review will make a difference to their everyday actions, in the same way that the possibility of recourse to formal judicial process serves usually to restrain within the law the activities of those who wield the power of the State. Such open processes probably also incline institutions to pursue consensual and inclusive solutions to their problems of coordination, rather than conflictual and exclusionary ones, since they are obliged periodically to confront the full range of outlooks and interests found within their boundaries. Such review processes may also serve to elaborate the values held by a specific occupational community, and provide occasion for strengthening the basis of normative commitment on which its work is based. A society integrated by 'communitarian' values and norms requires procedures, and indeed rituals, by which these can be explored, elaborated, and made the objects of agreement and commitment. (This model of deliberative review is set out in greater detail, with a proposal for its possible use in the school system, in Rustin, forthcoming.)

SOCIAL AND ECONOMIC RIGHTS AND THE CONSTITUTION

I have argued above that social and economic rights may be more susceptible of judicial definition and enforcement than some writers on citizenship have suggested. I have suggested that citizens might be more fully empowered both in individual capacities, to ensure that the State meets appropriate standards in the services it provides in return for its compulsory levies and contraints on citizens, and in collective ways, through the procedures for deliberative monitoring and review suggested. A new role for citizens, akin to that of jury service, is proposed, as members of regular review bodies examining the work of public agencies of many kinds.

However, there is a larger question behind all this. How far should social and economic rights (to work, to minimum incomes, to adequate shelter, to education, to health care, to safe environmental standards) be enforced by law, and be the objects of campaigns concerned in general with the rights of the citizen? Many of these proposed rights entail corresponding obligations (for example, in the case of a right to work, or to minimum income, or even to recieve education), but this does affect the present argument.

My argument is that it is regressive to advance definitions of and claims to citizenship which ignore these social and material dimensions. Charter 88, for example, should encourage discussion and debate about this wider agenda of rights, even though the amendment and enlargement of the Charter would have to depend on the outcome of such debates. It is mistaken to consider the rules of the political realm in isolation from the broader norms and rules governing social life, which the campaigns for constitutional reform currently do.

How far such social and economic rights may properly be incorporated into a written constitution is a different question. It seems unavoidable that any reference to such social rights as these in a constitution would be very general and abstract, merely the basis for detailed and contingent enactment in legislation. Still, a constitutional commitment to the economic well-being of citizens, to their nurturance in health by their community, to their access to education and useful employment, would at least signal a concern to meet the real rather than merely formal preconditions of citizenship. In a similar way the Social Charter proposed by the European Commission has proposed some minimum basis of occupational or industrial citizenship, without apparent conceptual or constitutional difficulty or anomaly. It is odd, in seeking a 'new constitutional settlement', to ignore (except in a few gestures towards a larger debate) all those issues of social justice, between classes, genders, and races, which have been central to the radical redefinition of citizenship in the twentieth century.

NOTES

1. Adults excepting women under thirty obtained the right to vote in 1918; women under thirty in 1928.
2. On the inflection of the agenda of the post-war welfare state by women, see Walby, S. (1989), pp. 165–8.
3. These debates are reviewed briefly in Rustin (1989). The 'failed bourgeois revolution' thesis was first argued by Anderson (1964) and subsequently developed by Nairn (1981). Later work by Stone and Fawtier Stone (1984) and by the conservative historian Jonathan Clark (1985) gives further indirect support to this argument. See also Barnett (1982) for the thinking on these issues of the coordinator of Charter 88. Therborn (1977) discusses the broader connections between democracy and capitalism, and Gamble (1988) examines the relation of State and economy under the Thatcher governments.
4. A collection of essays which has interesting suggestions on both these themes is Clode, D. et al. (1987).
5. The diffuseness of such services is the reason often given for the necessity of their regulation by professional bodies, or for their being provided by not-for-profit rather than profit-making organizations. But it is here seen as an argument for greater citizen involvement in defining and maintaining their standards. On this issue, see Powell (1987).

REFERENCES

Anderson, P. (1964) 'Origins of the Present Crisis', *New Left Review*, 23, Jan–Feb.

Barbalet, J. M. (1988) *Citizenship*.

Barnett, A. (1982) 'Iron Britannia', *New Left Review*, 134, July–Aug (reprinted Verso, 1983).

Bauman, Z. (1988) 'Is There a Postmodern Sociology?' *Theory, Culture and Society*, vol. 5, 2–3.

Clark, J. C. D. (1985) *English Society 1688–1832*.
Clode, D., et al. (1987) *Towards the Sensitive Bureaucracy*.
Corrigan, P. and Sayer, D. (1985) *The Great Arch*.
Gamble, A (1988) *The Free Economy and the Strong State*.
Giddens, A. (1972) *The Class Structure of the Advanced Societies*.
Great Britain (1988) *Education Reform Act*.
Great Britain (1989a) *Working for Patients* (White Paper on the Health Service, Cm 555).
Great Britain (1989b) *Caring for People* (White Paper on Community Care, Cm 849).
Great Britain (1990) *Supervision and Punishment in the Community* (Green Paper, Cm 966).
Hirschman, A. (1970) *Exit, Voice, and Loyalty*.
Le Grand, J. and Estrin, S. (1989) *Market Socialism*.
Marshall, T. H. (1950) *Citizenship and Social Class and other Essays*.
McCarthy, T. (1978) *The Critical Theory of Jürgen Habermas*.
Miller, D. (1989) *Market, State and Community: Theoretical Foundations of Market Socialism*.
Nairn, T. (1981) *The Break-Up of Britain*.
Nove, A. (1983) *The Economics of Feasible Socialism*.
Powell, W. W. (ed.) (1987) *The Nonprofit Sector*.
Pusey, M. (1987) *Jürgen Habermas*.
Rustin, M. J. (1985) 'A Statutory Right to Work', *For a Pluralist Socialism*.
Rustin, M. J. (1988) 'Full employment or post-employment?', *Critical Social Policy*, 22, Summer.
Rustin, M. J. (1989) 'A Constitution for a Pluralist Democracy?' in Alcock, P. et al., *The Social Economy and the Democratic State*.
Rustin, M. J. (forthcoming) 'Life Beyond Liberalism? Individuals, Citizens and Society', in Osborne, P. (ed.), *Socialism and the Limits of Liberalism*.
Stone, L. and Stone, J. Fawtier (1984) *An Open Elite? England 1540–1880*.
Therborn, G. (1977) 'The Rule of Capital and the Rise of Democracy', *New Left Review*, 103, May–June.
Walby, S. (1989) *Theories of Patriarchy*.

6 New Forms of Democracy for Socialist Renewal

Hilary Wainwright

'Stalinism is dead; long live socialism' is the toast we would *like* to make to the 1990s. But it's not the kind of slogan you would see sprayed on the walls of Warsaw, Budapest or Bucharest. In Prague, Berlin, Moscow and Vilnius – cities with pre-Stalinist socialist traditions – you might, if you search, find such a hope cautiously expressed. The question has to be faced of how socialism as a process and a project of popular self-emancipation can become sufficiently independent of 'actually existing socialism' to gain new life after the latter's collapse.

The movements in the East are first and foremost about democracy (although they draw an additional impetus from the widespread belief that democracy brings with it the private market and that, through this, consumption levels will rapidly rise). Twenty years earlier a Western revolt too, primarily against actually existing capitalism, but also rejecting the available models of socialism, made democracy its banner. There is no inevitability about a convergence between the aspirations of the two democratic revolts. But the renewal of socialism spurred on in the West by 1968 is not possible without the ideas now developing in the East, through the search – albeit only by a minority – for a path to democracy which will avoid the economic exploitation suffered in the West. Dialogue and debate between those making these different journeys is a condition for coherent principles that combine democracy and social justice. I want here to make some comments on one set of items on the agenda for such a dialogue: those items concerning the state's relation to society, including the sub-set of issues involved in the connections between representative and participative democracy.

My focus on democracy flows from a belief that the crisis of socialism is not the result of any exhaustion of the desire for social justice. It is rather the product of the failure of state institutions – the institutions historically associated with socialism – to bring social justice about and bring it about under the rule of the people.

Capitalism's reckless and exploitative drive to accumulate has been assailed from all sides: from the standpoint of women, blacks, dominated regions and suppressed nations, the victims of a collapsing eco-system as well as its traditional assailants at the point of production – all these, but rarely in the name of socialism. Socialism has historically associated the goal of social justice with the use by the working class and/or its representatives of state power. It is the viability of these means which are at a turning point, not the values of equality and social justice. (And, tangentially to my argument here: it is perhaps the absence of confidence about political means which turns each movement back on its own resources, giving an exaggerated sense of fragmentation and difference, compared with underlying values which are in fact frequently held in common.) It is this burning urgency of the problem of political means and mechanisms which leads me to consider issues of democracy to be central to the renewal of socialism.

My comments will draw from the experiences of social movements in the West, especially as they have come to engage with, and be in some way represented within, the political system. But, as if in a dialogue with members of equivalent movements in the East, I will try to address my comments to the broad conclusions that can be drawn from the experience of actually existing socialism in the East.

The prime demands of the movements in the East are for the basic conditions of representative government: freedom of association, free elections, a plurality of parties, and a free press. Without these basic rights of popular political expression and association, no sustained social advance is possible. The movements in the West have been able to take such formal rights for granted (and as a result have at times not been insistent enough that these achievements of liberalism, though insufficient, are nevertheless necessary for socialism). The impetus behind the growth of these Western movements has been disillusionment with the weak form of democracy that existing parliamentary institutions have allowed. As the expansion of education and the increased power of the workplace raised expectations of what it meant to be a citizen, many would-be citizens became aware of social and economic barriers to their full and equal participation.

The Western movements arising from this consciousness scrutinized and challenged the inequalities of social and economic power which coexisted with liberal democratic institutions. The force of their critique was that the wider context of political institutions which claim to be democratic must not only enable the conditions for democratic representation to be formally met, but must also make possible genuine popular sovereignty. The lesson from the experiences of the East is that a central state monopoly over economic planning and social provision is not compatible with meeting even the formal conditions of democratic representation. The only alternative in place is the domination of the private market. But the relations that this has produced historically, though compatible with a formal fulfilment of democratic representation, involve blockages to genuine rule by the people (as well as sometimes – notably but not exclusively, South Africa and until recently, Chile – suppressing basic democratic rights). I want to argue that the initiatives of recent social movements and associated parties, or sections of parties, in the West provide some pointers to new democratic forms. I will consider their contribution in relation to three problems for the political instruments of social justice: representation, administration and regulation. In each case I will start from a summary description of recent, usually localized, experiences in different West European cities, which illustrate ideas that need to be theorized and generalized. I cannot attempt here to carry out this generalization or even to deal with all the complexities raised by these local experiences, but I would argue that with sympathetic parties in government the kind of principles that they practice could be applied at a national level. The transformations set in motion would be revolutionary even if the means were, in one part, parliamentary.

POLITICAL REPRESENTATION

First, the problem of representation: theorists and practitioners of liberal democracy have argued that the representation of citizens as individual voters – each, it was presumed, with equal political weight – provided the truest feasible form of rule by the people, so long, that is, as the electoral system was fair – enabling each individual vote to count – and that the right to express minority opinions was protected. This is the belief to which many in the East, recoiling from state repression and the charade of elections for party monopolists, now turn. The experience of the real limits of representative government in the West, on the other hand, has led to popular initiatives – taken in part through electoral channels – which introduce new principles of representation. These principles are potentially complementary but also potentially in tension with existing parliamentary institutions. Two examples, one in England and the other in Germany, indicate both the new possibilities and the uneasy relations.

London 1984: the palatial concert room of County Hall has been taken over by the new Women's Committee of the Left wing Greater London Council for its first general meeting of women's groups London-wide. By the end of the evening the women have agreed to set up further more specialized gatherings: of women active in trade unions; black women; lesbians; older women; women with disabilities. In the months following this meeting these different groups of women elected representatives to sit with an equal vote to Councillors on the Women's Committee. These representatives, and the mass meetings of women's groups to which they were accountable, provided a direct link between the Women's Committee, potentially aloof in the fastness of the biggest regional government in England, and women's campaigns and struggles throughout London.

Frankfurt 1987: the basement of Frankfurt townhall, looking out into an attractive stone courtyard, has become a women's beer cellar for the day and 200 women from women's groups and projects have gathered to celebrate the election of a women's movement councillor (on the Green Party ticket) and the creation of a department for women in which women's groups will be directly represented.

Underlying these innovations is women's experience of the *gendered* character of existing political institutions. In pressing for a presence in the public political process as women's organizations they are saying, in effect, that this gender bias is more than a matter of the majority of existing representatives being men. This certainly *is* a problem, and many of these same women have been taking action to bring about change here too. Even massive increases, however, in the proportion of women politicians does not necessarily improve radically the state's ability to tackle the secondary position of women. Successful challenges to male political monopoly have not been invariably accompanied by effective challenges to the sexual division of labour throughout society. The Norwegian parliament, for instance, is made up of over 40 per cent of women. Between 1986 and 1989 over one third of the Cabinet were women, including the Prime Minister. Yet Norway has one of the most gender segregated occupational structures in Western Europe and child care provisions are amongst the lowest. This state of affairs did not improve significantly under the government of Gro Bruntland; and although her government was an accessible and benevolent one, full of good intentions, it was bound by conventional political forms. The idea of women's groups being in any way formally and publicly present was not even considered.

The women in Frankfurt and London by contrast are demonstrating in practice – even if not yet reflected in theory – the need for the economic and social struggles of women to be represented directly and democratically, through the women's groups which promote them, *in* the political decision-making process. In other words, these women, taking literally the commitment of radical politicians to women's rights, are saying that effective action to challenge women's subordination requires direct links with those already acting, independently of the state, to throw off their oppression. The practical outcome is experimentation in a new form of democracy. It combines the representation of individual but socially and economically unequal citizens with the representation of groups through which citizens organize to overcome their unequal social position.

What is the significance of this innovation? In these examples from the movements for the liberation of women, its importance stems from the social and economic roots of the gendered bias of political institutions. The interests and culture of male politicians have given this bias a momentum of its own; but its roots lie in the economic dependence (and often poverty) and continuing domestic burden of the majority of women. These fundamental features of women's secondary position have proved resistant to conventional forms of political change. The presence of women's organizations committed to striking at these foundations, directly in the political process, increases the possibilities – depending on their strength – of political institutions working in some partnership with struggles at the points where this subordination occurs. A similar partnership could be imagined with representatives of black organizations and trade unions. In the latter case it would in effect be a democratization, and radicalization, of the present secretive and bureaucratic involvement of the trade unions in the state machinery of social democratic government.

Why should such partnerships, in spite of their many problems, be necessary? *How* are they necessary? Part of the answer lies in the 'Heinekin principle'; the principle, borrowed from the beer advert. 'Heinekin: the beer that reaches the parts that other beers cannot) that there are parts of society that the state, even in socialist hands, cannot effectively reach, or at least cannot reach in an emancipating – as distinct from authoritarian – manner. Another way of putting this is to say that the status quo, whether the subordination of women or the exploitation of workers, depends on enduring social relationships, which persist because those within these relationships unwittingly reproduce them. A necessary, though often not sufficient condition – this is where the state comes in – for fundamental change, therefore, is action by those who suffer through these relations, to transform them. *In other words, social justice requires social movements, not simply to bring about a change in state power or to press for state action, but as an essential creative force in the process of change itself*.

Social movements however, without institutional support in the wider society, easily wax and wane; moreover a party in office can quickly forget its extra-parliamentary allies. One way of countering these tendencies and ensuring more favourable conditions for joint action between political institutions and social movements is for parties committed to social justice – socialist parties especially – to enable those social organizations that wish to, to have some direct input, locally and nationally, into the public political process. (This has interesting implications for the character of left parties and their relationship to social movements. Radical left parties, or groups within parties across Western Europe, are experimenting with new party forms – a process likely to be further stimulated by the experiences in Eastern Europe of movement/forum structures like New Forum in East Germany. This issue, however, requires separate analysis.)

NOT AS SIMPLE AS IT SOUNDS

My main intention in this essay is to draw attention to recent innovations in forms of representation, administration and social regulation arising out of recent social movements. Most innovations, however, reveal unanticipated problems – they would be very shallow innovations if they did not.

Political parties committed to being 'the voice of the movements' have found it to be a lot more complicated than simply getting on to the platform to speak. Movements are invariably divided and diffuse if, indeed, they can accurately be called 'movements'; the question of who has legitimate access to the political process and to representation within it has not been an easy question to answer. Such questions are not entirely new. In some form they have been raised constantly on the margins of the Labour Party, by radically minded trade unionists dissatisfied by the conservative, and in their view, undemocratic, way that trade unions are represented in the party. The new movements are putting these questions at the centre of strategies for social change.

The new movements, like the trade unionists involved in the formation of the Labour Party, are asserting that existing forms of citizenship are exclusive, based on inequalities of gender and race as well as class. But the new movements go further: the trade unions demanded to be present in the political processes because they believed – or at least the majority did – that government action could bring about the social changes they desired. (They saw their own role restricted to a limited area of bargaining.) The politics of the new social movements on the other hand – including innovative groups at the base of the unions – have been influenced significantly by disillusionment with political institutions and by a positive belief in social changes which they themselves have set in motion. Their involvement in the political system – a wary and yet a necessary one – is to gain access, resources and influence for their independent social base which, in spite of all its limitations, they believe is also a force for social transformation. Unlike the British trade unionists of the last eighty years they are not concerned to hand responsibility for social change to the politicians. This makes the partnerships that they have been creating – ad hoc and pragmatic as they are – more complex and the issue of representation and communication more vital. Both sides of the partnership are politically active; so representation must be such as to achieve the mobilization of their different sources of power, not simply to enable one partner to influence or pressure the other's exercise of power.

The roots of the problems of representation vary from movement to movement, depending on relations within the movements; on how far a movement really exists (in the sense of a common underlying direction) and on the character of competing claims to be the legitimate representatives. In relation to the trade unions, for instance, one problem has been a highly institutionalized gulf between full-time national leaders and lay workplace representatives. The outcome of past forms of trade union involvement in the political process has been trade union representatives closeted with ministers and civil servants with whom they are often far more in tune than they are with their members. Another problem for trade union involvement to bring about economic and industrial change rather than to manage the status quo, is whether trade union institutions, devised for the purpose of wage bargaining plus a little lobbying of the government, are sufficient for a trade union movement desiring to play a full part in a wider process of social change. The limited experience of political trade union initiatives (see the section later in this essay on 'social regulation') so far indicates the need for more direct connections between the political process and workers with a detailed knowledge of the industry or service for which they work.

The main problem which has arisen out of recent experience of women's representation has been a tendency for certain parts of the women's movement to claim exclusive moral legitimacy by virtue of their identity – as, for example, lesbians, black women, working class women – and to deny the competing claims of others of a similar identity but different politics. The basis for sustaining representation of a plurality of responses to a common oppression seems rarely to have existed and as a result the range of women participating in the political process has been far narrower than the objectives of the elected party would warrant.

The roots of this problem are deep and strong. They lie in women's necessary initial assertion of the reality of their distinct experience and the legitimacy of their feelings and judgement on this experience: its causes, its perpetrators, and the ways in which they might change it. This assertion was the groundspring of the women's movement. Such an assertion of the primacy of experience and the legitimacy of one's own subjective response to it is not unique to the women's movement. It is a feature of the early days of all movements of oppressed or marginalized people. Until that assertion is made, oppression goes unchallenged because the circumstances of the oppressed are taken for granted, assumed within the identity of dominant social groups, even by members of the oppressed group itself. A rebellion stems from circumstances which create a sense of a shared identity, an identity distinct and in some way opposed to the assumed identity imposed on, and previously absorbed by, the oppressed group; the momentum of resistance comes from this sense of a shared identity which is felt to arise from a common experience of a common oppression.

Experiences of particular oppressions differ. For instance, for some groups of people one complex of oppressive relations combines with another. The problem arises when a particular interpretation or response to the experience of oppression is held out to stand for, in effect substitute for, the experience of all those facing that oppression

– to stand, in fact, for the oppressed group as a whole. What is happening in such circumstances is that the early convergence of experience and subjective response is carried over by one section of the movement into a period when feelings and responses to a shared predicament have in fact diverged – as they inevitably will as a movement grows and faces differing circumstances, drawing in people from different backgrounds. The assertion of the primacy of felt experience at the beginning of a movement serves to open up a new social and political agenda, to provoke attention and to start debate about action. As the movement grows and different responses develop, the claim that one experience stands for the whole, that identity is in itself a sufficient argument, closes down debate, freezes the new agenda and narrows the basis for action. A party committed to overcoming social oppression, and understanding the importance of an active and respectful partnership with independent social movements, has to negotiate procedures and values to maintain an openness of debate between different parts of a movement committed to ending a common oppression. This process has hardly begun; for some time it was sufficient for radical left parties simply to proclaim themselves 'the voice of the movements'. Now that the movements have many different, conflicting thoughts to voice, the question of their political representation requires a more sophisticated answer.

THE LASTING INNOVATION

In spite of these unresolved questions, the examples of women's organizations with a foothold in the political system illustrate a principle which is, perhaps, the lasting innovation of the movements sparked off by the events of 1968. What these movements have established is the importance of social organization, *independent of the state*, oriented towards transforming existing social relations and in the process creating new ones. The experience of movements in Eastern Europe fighting for the social space to exist autonomously from the state dramatically underlines the importance of this principle. Implicitly, it redefines 'the social' in a way which does not equal – as in much socialist discourse and practice it has come to – the state. It thereby challenges the state monopoly over the meeting of social needs; and makes possible a *variety* of possible interconnections and combinations between different kinds of social action, including different levels and different forms of state action. Important new combinations can be seen in the administration of public resources. This is the second problem of the political instruments of social justice that have been, implicitly at any rate, addressed by the initiatives of recent social movements. Two projects, one in Sweden and one in England, illustrate some of the ways in which these movements have an impetus towards forms of democratic self-management.

THE ADMINISTRATION OF PUBLIC RESOURCES

Along one side of the square of a modern estate of blocks of flats in Göteborg, Sweden, is the long low building of the Women's Folk High School. One hundred adult women attend at any one time with seventeen staff; it is also much used for short courses and women's conferences. It was founded by a feminist group that came out of the Women's Liberation Movement of the early 1970s. It is funded by grants from the local, regional and national state but managed independently by a group of women from the Göteborg women's movement, with a range of sympathetic women on the school board. The board is responsible for a budget of nearly £1m. The women responsible – the staff, students and women from other women's projects in the city – run the school on principles of participative democracy, developed in the women's movement but now being developed – sometimes with difficulty – for the self management of a permanent and flourishing institution.

In Waterloo, down by the river Thames, surrounded by the high-rise tower blocks of the encroaching City of London, are the attractive houses, garden, shops and workshops of the Coin Street Development. Since the early 1970s the Coin Street Action Group had fought with every conceivable weapon, from street action to the law courts, to save their community from City property developers who would raze it to the ground. The arrival in 1982 of a sympathetic administration at London's County Hall laid the basis for victory. The GLC used its planning powers to buy the site from the property developers. The conventional procedure for a socialist municipality would then be to manage and develop the new acquisition exclusively through its own planning department, with a little consultation with the community, perhaps. Instead, the GLC negotiated an arrangement whereby the site would be managed, within certain agreed standards, by the Coin Street Action Committee itself. The GLC provided grants and expertise for the development of the site but the plans and their implementation were finally decided by local people.

Although these initiatives and many like them arose from very particular circumstances, they point to principles relevant to a general problem. The problem is this: as the state in most West European countries took over the provision of an increasing range of activities necessary to the supply and quality of labour, the administration of these services tended, for good or ill, to take on a life of its own. On the one hand, these activities were removed from the crippling commercial constraints of the market place. On the other hand, their ultimate accountability to parliamentary representatives could not provide the detailed stimulus and discipline necessary to respond adequately to people's changing needs and desires. Intermediate forms of democracy – generally more participative than representative, but involving some combination of the two – which bring together workers and users of the service, with some involvement from representatives of the state (at the appropriate level), provide a non-market answer to the bureaucratic tendencies inherent in the present administration of public provision.

There are no single models for these new democratic means of administration but it is possible from experience to point to certain necessary conditions. First, that the organizations primarily responsible for the management of the service have their own roots, independent of the state, in the community whom the service is intended to serve. Secondly, that they have the right and capacity to self management within a broad framework of standards and structures negotiated with the appropriate level of elected political representatives – national, regional or local. These conditions are necessary, not simply to live up to some kind of democratic virtue but because it is the participation of the users and direct providers of a service in its organization that could make it qualitatively more responsive to people's complicated and changing needs.

This form of organization improves the way that needs are identified. Knowledge of needs requires the interplay of two kinds of knowledge: the knowledge which comes from direct experience, and the knowledge which comes from specialized expertise. The two will often be in tension and contestation, which is why the Women's High School's ability to involve the students – with their direct experience of what they needed – as well as the adult education teachers – with their professional expertise – and board – with another combination of expertise and experience – in the running of the school is so important to its success.

Secondly this form of popularly based administration of public resources enriches the way that needs are met, in several ways. In Coin Street and at the Göteborg Women's High School, more or less everyone involved in providing a service or contributing to the provision of the services understands how all the different people and activities contribute to the overall character of the project. And since such activities usually do in fact depend on each other, an understanding of the overview by all those involved – normally a view exclusively available from the top – usually makes for a more responsive and creative capacity to meet people's needs.

PROBLEMS OF POWER AND WEALTH

These are local examples where social movements have been sufficiently self confident and powerful to carry out positive innovations towards the more democratic management of public resources. But they presuppose another kind of political power – at a local, national and increasingly in the future, international level – of a controlling and often confrontational kind, to obtain these resources for public use in the first place. In Sweden public resources are available for a project like the Women's High School – even if it takes a struggle with the state to release them – because of high taxes on profits and incomes. And these taxation levels along with other progressive features of Swedish society – the extent of trade union and government influence on private sector corporations for instance – are the product of a period of immense labour strength in the 1930s which led to a settlement unique in Western Europe. It was a settlement which, while saving the life of private capital, subjected it to severe constraints both from trade unions and from an extraordinarily well entrenched Social Democratic government. Those leaders of other West European Social Democratic or Labour Parties who point so favourably to 'the Swedish model' forget that its achievement and probably its spread was, and would be, the outcome of a trade union militancy on a massive scale that they pray nightly will never return. Similarly the possibility of the Coin Street Development Project depended on the GLC applying its planning powers to buy out the private property developers, against their will, and then on its drawing on a redistributive financial base to provide the projects' initial funding.

A DUAL APPROACH

These examples illustrate a dual approach to social transformation which has been absent from, or very subordinate to, socialist strategy ever since the first Socialist, Labour or Communist Parties gained office or power. In the early days of the socialist movement, the predominant polarization was between those who believed that socialism could be brought about through parliament and those who believed that, except for the occasional tactical use of parliament as a platform, socialism could only be achieved by mass, extra-parliamentary and eventually insurrectionary, action. There was a minority who believed in some combination, but the interconnections they envisaged were vague: little more than extra-parliamentary pressure behind a parliamentary leadership.

The recent social movements were born out of the experience, mainly negative, of social democratic governments. What is distinctive about the initiatives of these movements in relation to the state is that not only do they exert popular pressure – like any extra-parliamentary movement – but from a base outside the state they use its resources and legislative levers. In effect they are turning to new purposes some of the achievements of social democratic parties in ways which these parties, from their position so tightly within the state, were themselves incapable of. In a modest way they have used the small amount of political space which these gains made possible to pre-figure deeper forms of emancipation. They are demonstrating – often on a small scale because the power of movements and their political allies has been limited – that under certain conditions, state and popular action can combine to achieve social justice.

REGULATION

The third kind of political action where we have glimpsed, in recent popularly based initiatives, the possibility of more effective and more democratic instruments of social justice is in the direct regulation, control and socialization of private capital. Here the crucial issues are power and knowledge. Workers, on the inside of production, frequently have these in ways that no government, however well-intentioned, can have.

The examples of popularly based initiatives that I have drawn on so far come mainly from the experience of the 'new' social movements, particularly the women's movement. But the same approach can be found in practice, however untheorized, amongst the more innovative sections of the trade unions in Western Europe, especially in taking their own action to implement government-promised restraints against private capital.

The 'new social movements' are often counterposed to the 'traditional labour movement'. But in reality they are not comparable: the labour 'movement' has produced what are now, in fact, established institutions – the trade unions – within which the 'new movements', or the factors which produced these movements, have had as considerable an influence as they have within other established institutions (universities; schools; local government; the health service, and so on).

It is a little-noted fact that the new movements have significant roots – not just after-effects – within the institutions of labour. In England, for instance, the strike of women at the Fords auto company and the subsequent campaign for equal pay was a notable inspiration to the early women's liberation movement. And as if to reciprocate, socialist feminists in the late 1970s and 1980s played a vital role in organizing education for women trade unionists, and in setting up women's sections which forced issues of child care, working time, and other changes in the relation between work and personal life on to the agenda for trade union action. Legislation for equal pay proved worthless without such action. On issues of ecology and peace, the movements which burgeoned in the 1980s had in their early days been inspired by the innovative plan of a group of engineering workers at Lucas Aerospace, to turn the military production in which they were involved to the production of means for waste disposal, energy conservation, public transport, aids for the disabled and other socially useful mechanisms. Their plan arose out of a debate on whether they should call for the nationalization of Lucas Aerospace. After the experience of earlier nationalizations, they believed that nothing much would change unless they, the workers – working with politicians and organizations related to the potential users of their products – knew how to change the *purpose* and the *organization* of production. Their approach has spread: to local government in England, and to the metalworking unions of West Germany, Italy and Sweden.

These examples illustrate a further dimension of 'the Heinekin principle'. A further part that the state, however firmly controlled by a socialist government, cannot directly reach is the actual labour and technology of production. Yet the way production is organized effects virtually every other dimension of human life, through its importance for the distribution of wealth, the division of labour and labour time, the balance of power and the quality of the human and natural environment. The sorry fate of those attempts at socialist transformation that have ignored this limit on the state's capacities provide a negative proof of the argument. The Soviet state, for instance, was doomed from the moment it crushed the vulnerable shoots of worker's self management. In doing so it destroyed the one mechanism which, once developed, could release the skills, knowledge and power necessary for economic dynamism and technological innovation to underpin sustained social justice. In the West social democracy has never taken the opportunities, offered by periods of workers' militancy and self confidence, to forge an alliance based on these workers' understanding and power within the production process to reconstruct industry to meet social ends. Social Democratic and Labour Parties have related to the unions only as sources of electoral support and potential causes of inflation. As a result, interventions in industry have tended to be through the existing management and have brought about little change. The few exceptions, for example the Health and Safety legislation of the 1975–9 Labour Government in Britain, prove the point. the latter example had an impact because it empowered workers' organizations to implement the legislation, against the dictates of management. Industrial democracy within the framework of regional and sectoral planning is the only viable alternative to the blindly competitive drive to accumulate. Without it the economy stagnates and the technology becomes baroque.

INSTRUMENTS FOR SOCIAL JUSTICE

The case I am developing from the recent experiences of social movements and associated political parties in Western Europe has two main implications for the political instrument of social justice. On the one hand, it implies a democratic state: a state which is not only based on fair systems of representation but where this representation is all powerful, subject only to the safeguards of a written constitution and entrenched human rights, protected by a specially elected judiciary. This involves an elected assembly governing a state apparatus, in which nothing is secret; whose relations with different interests in society are transparent and accountable; whose military wing is under direct political control. This democratic vision is the immediate goal of movements in the East but it is still unfinished business in the West, where the imperatives of the Cold War and of capital's mobility have blocked the realization of such institutions. Such a political system is not socialism, but it is a precondition for socialism. Moreover, in many of the major West European powers it will only come about if popular pressure of almost Czechoslovakian proportions exerts itself for social and economic changes – changes that have been historically opposed by Western political establishments. The second implication is the importance, simultaneously, of creating the conditions for socialist and other radical, progressive parties (for example, the Greens) to share power, in the ways I have illustrated, with organizations rooted amongst those whose lives are presently constrained by exploitation or domination.

In Eastern Europe, socialism has been tried through one route: the exclusive use of the state in the hands of parties claiming to represent the working class, and has failed. The late nineteenth century craftsman, William Morris, described this process of trial and error in the cause of emancipation in *The Dream of John Ball*. John Ball felt that his labour would not be in vain if the people continued to strive for social justice. But he is not sure that they will. 'Is it so that they shall?', he asked anxiously; to which Morris replies, 'Yes, and their remedy shall be the same as thine, although the days be different: for if the folk be enthralled, what remedy save that they be set free? and if they have tried many roads towards freedom, and found that they led nowhither, then they shall try another'. Since 1968, long before failure led to the dramatic collapse we have witnessed in 1989, a myriad of different organizations, sharing the values for which socialism originally stood, have been paving the pathways of another route in the West (and in the South, though these experiences – in Nicaragua and Brazil – deserve full discussion in themselves). The connecting roads have still to be built and the signposts decided upon. Now in Europe, at least, it is through dialogue and co-operation with movements for democracy and social justice in the East that we can best clear away the (vast) remaining difficulties.

NOTE

I am grateful to Roy Bhaskar and Sheila Rowbotham for comments on the first draft of this article.

7 Equality and Difference: the Emergence of a New Concept of Citizenship

Anne Showstack Sassoon

A CLASSIC DILEMMA

Intellectuals, whether they try to intervene in politics or set their agenda for intellectual work on the basis of pre-constituted academic debates, face a constant danger of being cut off from reality. Confronted by the hurly-burly of events, buffeted about by political argument, intellectual discourse can all too easily be out of touch, lose its bearings, and seek an anchor in abstract schema which promise to order reality. In searching for the security blanket of correct ideas, it is so easy to lose sight of the concrete altogether, to remain behind the times, to lack a comparative historical or international perspective, to rationalize away pieces of the puzzle which do not fit neatly. Is it possible that our alienation from the mass of the population derives not only from the incomprehension which accompanies the distance between different skills and languages, but from the gulf between our work and the problems of daily life?

REAL LIFE AND NEW THINKING

An inescapable dimension of the challenge to socialist politics going back to the 1970s, which has culminated with the events of the last few months and years in Central and Eastern Europe, is the necessity of reconsidering our relationship with a tradition of political thinking. The word necessity is used advisedly, for the rethinking which we must undertake is rendered necessary by the changes of the present period. It is not an optional extra. It is not just a response to the politics of the right but to socio-economic change. What follows is prompted by trying to think through some of the theoretical implications of changes in women's socio-economic role, which provides a particularly useful window on a fundamental re-structuring of the relationship between different spheres of society. The fact that most women for most of their lives, including the period when they have full adult caring responsibilities, are in the formal labour force is a novelty which challenges the adequacy of the concepts at our disposal for analyzing the reality before us. We begin to appreciate how, for example, the conceptual division between public and private becomes all the more ephemeral when we examine the empirical complexity in contemporary society of the interdependence between the needs of the household, the world of work, and state policy. It is 'real life' which forces us into a new way of thinking.

What is being put into question is our *relationship* with traditional political thinking. What we have to consider is *how* to relate to the past. As the socialist regimes crumble, as democratic socialist parties, whatever they call themselves, attempt to reconstitute a basis of support in different countries, as the old statist solutions prove manifestly inadequate for the needs of daily life, a critique of Marxism has widely resulted in throwing away one tradition and has been accompanied, particularly, but not only, in the Anglo-Saxon world, by a renewed interest in liberal political thought. After years of intense theoretical debates informed by Marxism, or a version of it, in which other traditions were either ignored or dismissed, and which seemed only to end up in blind alleys occupied by a few intellectuals, there is the sensation that perhaps what we needed was there all the time if we had just recognized it, and cast off the provincial influence of our leftist ghetto. And what was more natural as one set of ideas was put into crisis than to confound a critical-analytical discussion of traditional ideas and thinkers, be they Marxist or liberal, with an adoption *tout court* of an alternative approach?

What is at issue, I would suggest, is how to avoid being fettered by old concepts, however they are understood, and from whatever tradition, which prevent us from knowing reality and from posing those questions which are appropriate today, which derive from the most recent historical developments. And here I would argue that, if we do reread the liberal tradition in order to arrive at a better understanding of our present predicament and in order to develop our contemporary political thinking so as to intervene in the reality confronting us and to influence the outcome of events, we need to recognize the historical, concrete, and political nature of the concepts we are dealing with. This is a contentious issue, given a history of superficially dismissing 'bourgeois ideas'.[1] However, far from reducing a tradition to its historical period or to the 'needs of capitalism', we can both better understand our task and learn from that tradition if we are more sensitive to the historical dimensions of the ideas we inherit.

When Hobbes, Locke, or others wrote, they, too, tried to produce concepts which were useful in intervening in the reality confronting them, in a moment when the existing political traditions no longer seemed to provide the framework for posing the classical political questions because of concrete social, economic and political change. We cannot fully appreciate their ideas, the contribution they made to their time and which they might made to ours, if we do not introduce this historical and political dimension. This is one aspect of understanding how they advanced political thought. It is much more than an academic question, for if we are to learn from them, we must be equally sensitive to the need to arrive at concepts which are adequate for our period. In asking questions about the elements of continuity with the past and in trying to ascertain those which indicate fundamental change, in trying not to lose an historical sense while our focus is on the present, we must be able to live the uncertainty of not being able to rely on *any* pre-existing schema while at the same time seeking to learn the lessons of thinkers from the past, of any tradition.

And here I think we can *also* learn from the way that thinkers like Marx and Gramsci approached their intellectual work. We could do well to pose some of the same questions which they posed, however critical we may be of the answers they arrived at. For example, a question which we, too, could ask is what messages do the major socio-economic changes of the day carry for rethinking politics? Further, how can we disarticulate the forms of these changes, which are specific – say, to Britain under Thatcher as compared to another country with a different history, a different culture and a different balance of political forces – from long term trends which can tell us about the potential of a whole period of historical change?

The first lesson which we can try to learn in reconsidering our relationship with the various traditions of political thought is the 'not to be taken for granted' nature of the questions before us, however obvious they may seem, and the productiveness of allowing the uncertainty, ambiguity, and discomfiture inherent in a period of transition and crisis, in which reality seems all too often out of our control or influence, to serve as the humus of the creative development of new thinking, informed but not trapped by the past. The knowledge we eventually arrive at is likely to be of a higher quality if we give ourselves permission to be tentative, acknowledge that knowing reality is an art as well as a science, and recognize that the pieces that do not slide easily into our old categories, or, to mix metaphors, the historical slips of the tongue, might well contain the seeds of new understanding.

CIVIL SOCIETY AND CITIZENSHIP

In recent years the concepts of civil society and citizenship have gained a prominent place in debates on the left in Britain. An associated concept but one which has not occupied the same prominence, probably connected with the undermining of the post-war consensus, the political ascendency of the right, and the development of the 'two-thirds, one-third society', but which is in fact integral to these notions, is the liberal concept of equality. It is important to bear in mind that these ideas not only have a history as ideas but cannot be dissociated from a whole historical epoch, the development of modern, post-feudal society and the modern state in which we can begin to talk about different public and private spheres with all that that implies. This allows us to comprehend their novelty in their own time, to analyze their utility today and to understand the concrete historical and political reasons why we are still obliged to make reference to them. If concepts like civil society and citizenship cannot be 'put in the loft',[2] as historically outmoded ideas, it is for very real reasons. And yet, for other equally real, concrete reasons, we cannot simply adopt them as an alternative to the impoverished thinking which has so long dominated left political discourse. Contemporary conditions require us *both* to use these concepts as they acquire new meaning *and* to go beyond them.[3] If, for example, we historicize and make concrete the concept of citizenship, we would have to examine the terrain on which it is exercised today. That terrain includes the welfare state. And what comes into play is a highly complex and differentiated relationship to the state, mediated through a wide range of institutions, in which the differences between people, according to resources and needs, family situation and point in the life cycle, and life history with regard to the world of work are as significant as equality before the law or equal political rights.[4]

The abstract nature of recent discussions about the concepts of civil society and citizenship, although responding to a very real political context, has occluded the possibility of these concepts being enriched to make them more useful for us today by rooting them in their concrete terrain. This is by no means to diminish the importance of insisting on the need for legal guarantees and protection of civil liberties in the context of an erosion of civil rights. One aspect of the abstract and general nature of much of this debate is that questions of race and nationality have not had a weight adequately reflecting the effects of government policy on the ethnic minorities, a comment undoubtedly on a left which is so often 'hard of hearing' with regard to the claims of these groups. At the same time the extensive and rich feminist literature offering a critique of an ungendered concept of citizenship finds no echo in the dominant debate. Nor have civil rights been redefined to include social citizenship rights or what have been called the rights of daily life.

Current interest in the concept of civil society in Britain is in part a response to the reorganization of the state–society relationship under Thatcher, which is being paralleled in different forms throughout Europe. But the debate has also been spurred by developments in Eastern Europe, where the concept of civil society has served such an important political purpose deriving both from its analytical function and its normative claims.[5] To a lesser extent, the renewed interest in the possibilities of a regenerated and empowered civil society in the West is informed by the awareness that the fight for a progressive politics cannot take the form of a defence *tout court* of the welfare state and traditional social democracy. This is in part because after more than ten years of Thatcher, three electoral defeats for the Labour Party, and profound socio-economic change, in Britain as throughout Europe, society is not what it was.

Yet there is a danger in the way the terms of much of the discussion have been posed. Again, they have been abstract, not rooted in what is happening in society. For ironically, in focusing on the political form of changes, that is, on the way this period has been moulded by a particular kind of politics, the political implications of underlying socio-economic trends, for example, the increased participation of women in the labour force, or the increasing complexity of individual and social needs, have often been obscured. That is, the significance of the complex dynamic and organization of society in impinging on the role of the state or, put differently, the *necessity* of rethinking the role of the state derived from these underlying changes, which are not caused and cannot be controlled by any political force, has tended to be obscured. Thus while there has been some acknowledgement of the need to re-think the role of the state, it has in the main been in answer to a political and ideological offensive and consequently has assumed a defensive character, 'we, too, are critical of the state'. It has not been derived from an analysis of the implications of socio-economic conditions. It has not reflected an awareness that we are in fact *constrained* to rethink the state as society changes. To this extent it has, in fact, failed to replicate an important dimension of the tradition of political thought which we inherit.

Traditionally, going back to the classics of liberalism, but also to Hegel and the early Marx, the definition of civil society was always inter-related with an analysis of the emergence of the modern state. To cite a more recent example, Gramsci's argument that there is a potential for the expansion of civil society and the reduction of state power is rooted in the concomitant complexities and contradictions of the state and of civil society, as they *are*. In fact, Gramsci continues a long tradition of political thought when he asks, what do socio-economic changes tell us about what he calls the classic question of political science, of *any* political science, the division between leaders and led? And yet he goes beyond this tradition when he argues that for concrete, historical reasons – that is, because of the real development of society – a new, unprecedented question is on the historical agenda, the possibility of overcoming that division. Now this was a question which was also posed by Marx, but it was considered with new urgency by Gramsci for historical reasons, amongst which figure the first concrete attempt to build socialism, but equally, if not more importantly, for Gramsci the latest developments of capitalism. These are phenomena which make possible a further expansion and development of civil society, and an unprecedented development of democracy, at the same time as they posed concretely all the problems inherent in such a development.[6] Democracy was on the historical agenda despite the recomposition of relations of domination and subordination through what Gramsci terms the passive revolution evident in the policies of various regimes which subsume the progressive possibilities of the present moment.[7]

What is missing from today's debates is a parallel analysis of the potential and the problems inherent in the most recent developments of society, developments which are not due to the fact that one party or another is in power. The recent focus on civil society has tended to ignore, or at least to take for granted, the other side of the coin, the state, even though the condition of one implies the condition of the other and implicates a particular web of relations between the two. If, for example, there is a move away from an overly centralized, hierarchical, and bureaucratic organization of services throughout Europe and a recourse to new forms of social provision which override the bounds of private and public, if the state is assuming more an enabling role, then this is because the complexity and diversity of social needs *require* a new relationship between civil society and state. That is, any renewal of civil society of necessity implies the reconstruction of the state, not just less of it, but something different, with a different web of relations with society.

But what? It is, of course, easier to criticize 'the old' than to analyse 'the new' which is emerging. Perhaps, given the widespread disillusion with grand designs and with technocratic utopias, what the postmodernists call metanarratives, intellectual modesty is hardly misplaced. And it is also the case that our old conceptual spectacles allow us to see the old better than the new. Yet perhaps the task itself is misunderstood. If intellectuals are increasingly aware that they cannot spin utopias out of their heads, perhaps their vocation is to concentrate on trying to ask the right questions of what *is*, of what is already happening beneath our eyes if we could only see it, in order to understand the possibilities of what *might be*.

What possibilities, dilemmas and contradictions, for example, are contained in a major socio-economic change like the dramatic increase of women in the formal labour market or the complexities of meeting social needs in a modern welfare state? What does the dynamic of social reality tell us about concepts like civil society, state, citizenship, equality, difference, public, and private? Are the categories we possess adequate to capture the full potential of the dynamic of this pulsating, fragmented, contradictory society? How do we understand the objective and subjective aspects of phenomena which are the product of the decisions of millions of individuals, which are affected by public policy and therefore politics but which are outside of the control of any political force, whose forms vary from country to country because of different traditions, culture and institutional arrangements while manifesting similar patterns? How do we keep all the different perspectives in mind: the macro and the micro, individual choices and the policy decisions of state or economic entities, historical, cultural and national specificities and general, longterm international trends? Is it possible, for example, that by starting with an analysis of the material facts of millions of women combining the public and private spheres, family needs and participation in formal paid work, we are constrained to think in a new way about concepts like the individual, equality, and difference?

THE INDIVIDUAL, EQUALITY, AND DIFFERENCE

An important aspect of the debate about civil society is a reassertion of the civil role of individuals. Thus we arrive at another concept deriving from classical liberal political thought, the individual. The concept of civil society as it emerges from contract theory and liberal political thought cannot be separated from the notion of an autonomous, separate individual, a universal figure whose essence is defined in terms of his [sic] relation to the rule of law, whose equality stems from eliminating from this relationship all indications of social status, socio-economic position, race, gender, and so on. Hence the symbolism of justice blindfolded. Just as the emergence of civil society, the rule of law, and the modern state were a great advance in the period, the insistence on the universal aspects of the citizen detached from specificity and difference was an advance on the bonds of feudal society and traditional social relations in so far as status no longer determined the formal legal relationship between citizen and state.

The reality of this advance in its time is not negated by recognition of its gendered character, or by the fact that a new set of circumstances in turn leads to further advances and new contradictions. As legal and constitutional guarantees of civil rights were slowly established, the fight for an expansion of democratic political rights in turn opened up the possibility that the struggle for social reforms and for social citizenship rights could be placed on the political agenda as the political terrain was transformed by the expansion of the suffrage. What were previously defined as private needs could be articulated as demands addressed to the state because of a concomitant development. That is, the granting of political rights to individuals went hand in hand with the increasing weight in politics of organized groups, the right of association providing the possibility for individuals, at the same time, to enjoy a corporate presence in politics, as members of groups. Citizenship comes to signify both legal, constitutional representation of the individual, first men and then women, and *de facto* representation of organized groups. As the meaning of citizenship is expanded to include not only civil but political rights, the conditions are created for a major change. The concrete translation of civil and political rights into the articulation of social needs as demands on the state by political parties and pressure groups, and the resultant expansion of social policy and state intervention in society, creates a complex and contradictory picture in which the relationship between individual and state, and hence citizenship, is transformed both politically and socially with the establishment and expansion of the welfare state.[8]

What, then, are some of the ways in which the abstract concept of the individual, despite its limitations, still functions and why is it still necessary, or at least a version of it? The first thing to point out is that while ruling out of court the significance of difference, that is, while it is posed as universal and abstract, the notion of the individual implicitly also recognizes difference.[9] That is, it implies that human beings are separate and individual and act as such on the basis of different needs and different desires. It would be difficult to deny that there is a continuing necessity to assert the importance of what is an expression of the liberal notion of equality before the law, that is, equal opportunities, which is no more than the assertion that irrelevant differences should play no part in preventing individuals, *however different they are*, from competing with each other under the same set of rules. Thus here, too, in a similarly contradictory way, differences are recognized if only for their status and import to be relegated to the social sphere and subtracted from the application of the rules of the game, be it the law or the rules governing institutions such as in employment or education.[10] What is constituted is a hierarchy with the universal, the general, the abstract as dominant, and the particular, the concrete, subordinant, as threatening the social order if not kept within the bounds of the rule of law because individual needs were primarily viewed as separate and contradictory.

Yet if we consider these questions from a more recent point of view and make them concrete, we arrive at another dimension. From the perspective of the needs of the individual in contemporary society, in the context of the welfare state and with the increasing participation rate of women in the world of production, we arrive at a picture of complexity and social interdependence. In terms of the responsibility we each have as adults to care for ourselves and others, children, partners, parents, and to cover the myriad needs of households, at any one moment in time, the needs of one person are very different from another. In modern conditions of the welfare state and advanced industrial society, when both men and women are in formal, paid work, these differences have entered the public arena. They can no longer be conceptualized as private. In addition to being structured by gender and by contemporary forms of the sexual division of labour, in which women have the main caring responsibilities but in which they are also in the formal labour force, compared to earlier times, the fulfilment of needs and the definition of differences depend on a much more complex set of conditions and institutions, related both to the services which are available but also to the organization of work and of time.[11] Any concept of the individual adequate to contemporary conditions must of necessity include these complexities and these differences, in what we are and in what we need. Moreover, the highly mediated relationship between individual and state through a web of institutions, which overlap the bounds between civil society and state, puts into question much of the conceptual framework of liberal political thought posited on a direct relationship between individual and state *at the very same time* as other of its percepts such as the rule of law, founded on just such a direct relationship, are as significant and important as ever.

The concept of the individual can be viewed from still another perspective, using knowledge which goes beyond what was available earlier. Applying more modern insights coming from, for example, psychoanalysis, we are aware that concrete individuals, you and me, each have different life histories and both complex and evolving inner dynamics and identities (which can only in fact be understood as process). We are each different, we are each unique, however much we may have things in common, and however much the outsider, the professional, the intellectual might be able to discern patterns over time or across society. We have different points of view. However constrained by influences outside of ourselves, by institutions and practices, our subjectivity and identity are highly individual and complex.

On different levels, and from different perspectives, then, we need the concept of the individual, but this does not mean that the content of this concept can remain what it is in liberal political thought, or that the wide range of criticisms of this notion of abstract individual and of the concept of equality which accompanies it can be ignored. Perhaps the most familiar is an insistence on the social conditions which make it impossible for all individuals in fact to enjoy the full benefits of the protection of the rule of law and of civil rights because of the different resources, cultural as well as economic or social, which they possess. In addition, a Marxist approach would criticize the universality of the notion as ahistorical and as obscuring, for example, the inevitable structural imbalance of power between individuals who are, in fact, situated in classes, an imbalance which is imposed by the relations of production.

More recent anti-racist and feminist critiques lead us to new dimensions. These go beyond a claim for equal opportunities. They are informed by the recognition of the differentiated effects of an equal application of the rules to people who are different. On the one hand, this is because the rules themselves contain assumptions which are far from neutral or universal. On the other, the very notion of the universal in silencing differences in fact derives its very meaning from subordinating or marginalizing the other, the specific, the particular, the different.[12] On a concrete, practical level, equal achievement premised on integration into the dominant model is impossible. Consequently, these critiques assert the value and validity of different identities, of race, nationality, religion, gender.[13]

And something strange happens. While criticizing the abstract, universal dimensions of the concept, what takes place is a complex redefinition of the individual, as member of a group, a category, a gender, yes, affected by the rules in a particular way because of sharing certain characteristics with others, but whose identity is meaningful in so far as it is redefined in its concrete peculiarity and individuality, in its separateness, in its multidimensionality, in its moment, that is, its stage in the life cycle, its differentiated, specific, mediated relationship to the state. In a sense what we have in common is our separateness, our uniqueness, the fact that we are different, our sense of being alone. Disarticulating and making concrete the abstract concept of the individual helps us to recognize something else: viewed from one facet or another of our identity or our subjectivity,we each belong to a partial group, we are each an 'other', whatever our race, gender, nationality.

INTERDEPENDENCE, COMPLEXITY, AND A NEW CONCEPT OF CITIZENSHIP

What has been inserted into the political process is a contradiction which is a result of the expansion of democracy and the extension of civil rights. Combined with the need for greater state intervention as modern industrial society developed, as people fought for and gained the vote, and as they organized in parties, trade unions, and pressure groups, the old utilitarian aim of making the state responsive to people's desires took on a new meaning. The expansion of the welfare state was in part the result of the insertion on to the political agenda of a range of social needs. The relationship of the individual to the state began to be defined, in fact if not in words, both in terms of equality, equal treatment by the law, and in terms of difference, differentiation according to needs. I am a citizen of a state with certain rights. Those rights, civil, political, or social, in T. H. Marshall's perspective,[14] are the same for all citizens, but the needs of individuals vary enormously. From the point of view of the individual, as our needs, not just our resources, vary over the life cycle, so does our relationship to the state. And at any one moment, the citizenry at large has a highly differentiated relationship to the state.[15]

The contradiction has also been inserted into the world of production.[16] The principle of economic organization in the modern period, which applies both to socialism and to capitalism, is that the worker is paid for the job done, all differences being left behind. That is, there is a parallel with the principle of formal, legal equality, and there are also parallel criticisms of the gendered character of both the application of this principle in practice and the universality implied in it. Equal access to jobs and equal treatment at work is the ideal and the goal, the object of the fight for equality. If people have different needs outside of the world of work, they are supposed to be left behind, to be addressed through the market, the servicing work done by women, or the state. The organization of work is blindfolded, just like justice, as it is confronted by the concrete social figures who in fact bring with them a huge range of needs which are highly differentiated at any one moment and, for the individual, over the lifetime. This has always been the case in modern industrial society, but once these social figures are increasingly women, less and less can needs be said to belong to another sphere. The classic reserve army of carers, women, as they straddle work and private life, bring into the open a contradiction which was hitherto hidden by the sexual division of labour. Paid work impinges on their ability to satisfy social needs, and their responsibility for social needs both impinges on their lives in the productive sphere (and, consequently, their financial wellbeing whether from wages or benefits such as pensions related to history in the work force) and manifestly cannot and never has been consigned to the state or to the market.

What is immanent in the situation is the necessity of a transformation of the very logic of production in which Marx's definition of communism, 'from each according to his [sic] ability, to each according to his needs', is gendered, made concrete, no longer reduced to an economic calculation, and takes account of social organization. The centrality of paid work, the over-determination of our lives by rigid inflexible jobs, is being challenged. This is the context of a further redefinition of citizenship, of social rights, to include the rights of daily life and extended to the right, for men as well as women, of 'time to care'.[17] That is, if we look at even the most advanced welfare states, the Nordic countries, we cannot conceive of all caring needs being taken over by the state, the market, or even voluntary organizations in civil society. We need to be guaranteed time to care, and flexibility in our working lives – over the life cycle and in the organization of work and in social insititutions – to reflect a politics of time.[18] What is being asked of the state here is something traditional: legal regulation. But its object is novel and indicative of a new relationship between state and society, between the state and the individual: to enable, to facilitate our individual and social creativity. Changes of this nature are subversive of a whole order. They are revolutionary, but they are not utopian because they reflect real social needs manifest in the lives of millions of people.

From this perspective, the private, the social, the economic, the political, civil society and the state form such a web of interdependencies that it is difficult if not impossible to 'think' them separately. Yet if these categories, like the concept of citizenship, are still used and have a significance, and consequently are still necessary, changes in society, in daily life, mean that in fact they are being reformulated and enriched. Their increasing complexity reflects the complexity of society itself, of the daily lives of millions of people. To the extent they remain simple, general, ahistorical and abstract, they cease to represent this reality, rather like the intellectuals who use them.

The introduction of gender into our way of thinking undermines the universality of traditional conceptual schema. The rich intellectual production of feminists, which has placed gender on the intellectual agenda, is underpinned by the daily experience of millions of women who negotiate the various spheres of society as adults with full caring responsibilities, who nonetheless engage in formal paid work, with all the constraints this implies, whose lives are lived in institutions built on assumptions, values, symbols, often only implicit and therefore all the more undermining of our definition of self, which alienate and incapacitate us. What they – we – experience is the impossibility of women feeling at ease in a world made according to a male model.

What intellectual reflection has retrieved from obscurity is that this model is male in part because the public world has been shaped empirically by those social figures who have constructed it, men. But perhaps more significantly, in terms of any project of transforming the conditions of domination and subordination as they exist now and have existed over time, is the realization that our very conceptual framework and our symbolic order in the modern period provide a structure and a justification for these conditions. The political system, the world of work and theoretical discourse are all premised on a concept of the universal which maintains the pretence of being abstract and general. The way institutions are organized, the rules which govern their practices, our language and concepts (for example, the rights of Man), our notion of reason itself, present themselves as blind, just like justice, to gender, as they pretend to be universal.[19]

We can 'deconstruct' the pretence of the universal, and uncover this blindness and this silence, working from two perspectives, one historical and one ahistorical. As it has developed in modern, post-feudal and then industrial society, and given conceptual form in the Enlightenment, the pretence of blind, neutral universality has contributed to the concrete, historical subordination and marginalization of women, and legitimized the historical domination of men, the concrete figures who built the public sphere of institutions and concepts. The relegation by modern thought of the specific, the concrete, the other to a lesser status was part of an attempt to comprehend, order and control the jumble of reality through the establishment of general, universal categories. This project goes back to the Greeks but acquires a particular power with regard to the mass of the population as it informs a web of institutions which affect our lives intimately, as the universal, the general, moves beyond the province of philosopher kings to structure the thinking of civil servants, policy makers, and social scientists.

The inadequacy of modern, universalizing thought is further revealed by focusing on another aspect which is ahistorical: the fact that the world is made of two genders. What this means at any one moment in time, what it is to be female or male, their internal complexities, the interdependency between the definition of one and the other are historically, socially and culturally determined. The argument is not derived from biological essentialism. Biology is in any case but one aspect of a much more complex phenomenon, and its significance is transformed by social and technological change. The internal complexities of masculinity and femininity signify that we can never think one as the opposite of the other. Further, as we are each a different mixture of femininity and masculinity, but our identities are overdetermined by one or the other, it is impossible to conceptualize androgeny. But whatever this means at a particular moment in time or for a particular, concrete individual, however our gender identities are constrained, regulated, influenced by rules, norms, symbols, ideas, practices, related to our biological, bodily being or our social role, it follows as night follows day that the world has and always will have different genders.

The need to think gender, then, is not historical or political although it arises in a historical and political context. Although there may be concrete, historical and political reasons why it has been put on the table now, the need to conceptualize difference does not derive, for example, from a movement which manifests in the public arena a preconstituted set of differences, such as the working class. That is, it is not a constitution of an interest like other interests which may or may not be incorporated into the political system like economic or class interests have been. Instead it is derived, as argued above, from something much more fundamental. Our very identities are structured by gendered relations which permeate institutions and practices. No project of universalizing difference or mediating or reconciling conflicts based on difference is possible.

What is, however, on the historical agenda is another project – the construction of a terrain and the ideas and institutions and practices appropriate to it, in which differences and conflicts exist and are recognized and in which a dynamic, organic, differentiated concept of unity replaces the false premisses of traditional social and political institutions and practices. Concretely we have to think about how to create a woman-friendly world, in which women can be at their ease, a world made for women *and* men. A world which suits *two* genders could well mean overcoming not only the alienation of women, but also of men. To extend the discussion, we might also, for example, be able to *see* and give recognition to racial and ethnic differences, not as the other, the lesser, but as different, as we comprehend how we are each part of some minority. What is being inserted into the very foundation of politics is complexity and conflict, as the irreconcilable difference implanted in the gendered structure of our identities confronts the universalistic pretence of social and political institutions and theory. One inference is that the impossibility of women (or men for that matter) leaving their gender identity behind when they are actors in the public sphere be spoken and be given a status. That is, our identities as gendered beings need to be recognized to enable women to act in the public sphere as women, and not as surrogate men.

It is not surprising that there is great hesitancy to embark on this road. Difference *has* been spoken – in private, in the form of sexual stereotypes, as part of a public and private structure of domination and subordination. We are still wary because of the birthmarks of the painful struggle for equality. There is still the need to fight old, outmoded concepts of difference. But we must be under no illusions. The institutions and practices which bear the marks of the old are the product of the historical domination of one gender. The concept of the universal or the practices of these institutions which are incapable of speaking gender or difference construct the subordination of women. Blinding ourselves to difference does not mean that it ceases to exist. We will simply fail to comprehend why women remain subordinate in a world made for one gender, or to pose, whatever the social organization, the question of creating the conditions for an enriched, complex concept and practice of equality as the foundations are laid for the expansion of freedom of the individual as we escape the constraints of the universal. We arrive at the notion that, if the concept of universal equality before the law, in which irrelevant differences play no role, is manifestly still necessary both in terms of civil rights and equal opportunities, it rests alongside the necessity of thinking difference and specificity, a necessity imposed upon us by socio-economic change, the consequent transformation of social needs, articulated or not, in the new ways in which we articulate our subjectivity and perceive our identity, and advances in intellectual perception which render the notion of the individual both complex and problematic.

What we can observe are a variety of challenges to traditional political science and traditional politics, to the role of the intellectuals as experts and to social policy making. By introducing difference, complexity and conflict into the foundation stones of political and social theory and practice, the task of politics and of social policy changes. What is made necessary is a process in which differences and highly differentiated needs are addressed in their specificity and peculiarity, in which it is recognized that the universal can be as misleading as the specific, in which the need for rethinking the democratic process and democratic institutions derives from the very development of the modern period. We are experiencing the rearticulation of the meaning of the individual, and the emergence of a new concept of citizenship.

We are living in a period in which the old lines of public and private, of state and civil society, are being transformed whether we like it or not. Further, what are being scrutinized in new terms are the conditions in which women participate in public life, be it in the state, the productive, or the social spheres. The forms of transformations taking place between and within spheres differ from country to country according to historical and political traditions and according to the balance of political forces. Comprehending let alone intervening in this reality is a daunting task. Does abolishing the universal signify abandoning any attempt at general comprehension, as much of the debate on post-modernism would have it? Are we limited to partial, occasional, haphazard knowledge? Or are we forced to begin to construct a new way of thinking and of understanding reality in its complexity and diversity? If the task seems overwhelming, the brutal recognition of what is before us is but the first step to that moral and intellectual revolution which Gramsci maintained is at the heart of political change.

NOTES

1. It is also a contentious issue academically. Quentin Skinner's work, which emphasizes the importance of the historical context of the work of political philosophy, has provoked controversy in the Anglo-Saxon academic world.
2. This was what Benedetto Croce suggested should be done with Marxism at the end of the last century.
3. This is what Gramsci does with a number of concepts such as intellectual, civil society, state, hegemony. See Anne Showstack Sassoon, 'Gramsci's Subversion of the Language of Politics', in *Rethinking Marxism*, Spring 1990.
4. See Chiara Saraceno, 'La struttura di genere della cittadinanza', in *Democrazia e diritto*, no. 1, 1988.
5. See John Keane (ed.), *Civil Society and the State*, part 3, London, 1988 and Vera Gáthy (ed.), *State and Civil Society: Relationships in Flux* (Budapest, 1989) for a sample of some of this discussion.
6. See Anne Showstack Sassoon, *Gramsci's Politics*, 2nd edition (London, 1987).
7. See Ch. 13, 'Passive Revolution: a Strategy for the Bourgeoisie in the War of Position', in Sassoon, *Gramsci's Politics*, or a slightly extended version, 'Passive Revolution or the Politics of Reform', in Anne Showstack Sassoon (ed.), *Approaches to Gramsci* (London, 1982).

Also see Franco de Felice, 'Rivoluzione passiva, fascismo, americanismo in Gramsci', in Franco Ferri (ed.), *Politica e storia in Gramsci* (Rome, 1977); Christine Buci-Glucksmann, *Gramsci and the State* (London, 1980) Ch. 14; and Christine Buci-Glucksmann, 'State, Transition and Passive Revolution', in Chantal Mouffe (ed.), *Gramsci and Marxist Theory* (London, 1979).

8. I do not mean to ignore Foucault's argument or those of others about the constitution of relationships of power, of domination and subordination, through the establishment of modern state institutions and through the effects of social policy and the power of experts, or the influence, for example, in Britain of top level committees which justified the introduction of social reforms in terms, say, of guaranteeing a supply of healthy men for the armed forces. Regarding the latter, see Pat Thane, *The Foundations of the Welfare State* (London, 1982). I would simply stress the importance of a multi-dimensional analysis which avoids reducing the development of modern social policy to an expression of domination.
9. See Joan W. Scott, 'Deconstructing Equality-versus-Difference: or, the Uses of Poststructuralist Theory for Feminism', in *Feminist Studies*, no. 1, 1988. Carole Pateman's forceful critique of the liberal concept of the individual as constructing the suppression of women is useful but focuses on only one aspect: *The Sexual Contract* (Oxford, 1988).
10. The highly sensitive nature of the relationship between equality and difference and the continuing power of sexual stereotyping to justify discriminatory practices was illustrated recently in the United States in a case brought by the Equal Employment Opportunity Commission against Sears, Roebuck. Sears successfully defended employing women in certain lower paid jobs by relying on the testimony of one historian against another that women have historically chosen certain kinds of work. See Scott, 'Deconstructing Equality-versus-Difference', and Alice Kessler-Harris, 'Equal Employment Opportunity Commission v. Sears, Roebuck and Company: a Personal Account', in *Feminist Review*, no. 25, 1987. Alice Kessler-Harris was the historian who argued against the Sears position.
11. The Women's Committee of the Italian Communist Party has published an interesting document which develops these themes and which reflects a widespread discussion amongst Italian feminists on the questions of difference and the politics of time. It has been widely debated inside and outside the party, and the debate has caused a marked shift in the terms of reference of the Italian left. Sezione femminile della Direzione del PCI, *Dalle donne alle donne. Carta itinerante* (Rome, 1987).
12. The poststructuralist and postmodernist literature on this is immense. For a good summary of some of the important arguments see Scott, 'Deconstructing Equality-versus-Difference'.
13. The feminist critique, of course, is not identical with and is not even always parallel to the insights coming from a discussion of race and ethnicity, and it would be important to investigate the differences. Amongst the by now large body of literature which challenges feminist

work to go beyond ethnocentricity, an article which I found particularly stimulating is Chandra Mohanty, 'Under Western Eyes: Feminist Scholarship and Colonial Discourses', in *Feminist Review*, no. 30, 1988.

14. See T. H. Marshall, 'Citizenship and Social Class', in *Sociology at the Crossroads* (London, 1963).

15. The public/private dichotomy itself varies at any one time for different groups in the population. Whereas once those who did not have sufficient property or were of the wrong gender could not vote and therefore did not have a public role so that they were confined to a 'private' life, now the poor in many countries hardly enjoy a private sphere at all as the most intimate details of their lives are subject to public scrutiny. Saraceno extends some of Habermas's ideas in this regard in 'La struttura di genere della cittadinanza', p. 285.

16. I discuss the ideas of this section, as well as issues relating to the welfare state, at greater length in 'Women's New Social Role: Contradictions of the Welfare State', in Anne Showstack Sassoon (ed.), *Women and the State. The Shifting Boundaries of Public and Private* (London, 1987).

17. Sweden has produced a report on the implications of this perspective for social policy. See Marten Lagergren, et al., *Time to Care* (Oxford, 1984). The Nordic discussion has had a significant echo in Italy. See Laura Balbo and Helga Notwotny (eds), *Time to Care in Tomorrow's Welfare Systems: the Nordic Experience and the Italian Case* (Vienna, 1986).

18. A campaign for a law along these lines which provides, amongst other things, for extensive parental leave, a reduction of the working week to 35 hours, one year's leave every seven, and gives power to local authorities to change the schedules of shops, services, and other sectors to suit better the needs of private life, is being conducted in Italy by the Women's Committee of the PCI.

19. On the relationship between the concept of reason as it has developed historically and gender see Genevieve Lloyd, *The Man of Reason. 'Male' and 'Female' in Western Philosophy* (London, 1984). See also Sandra Harding, *The Science Question in Feminism* (Milton Keynes, 1987). In France the work of Hélène Cixous and Luce Irigaray has been very important in this discussion. Irigaray has been influential in Italy. The Italian debates, which have been more political, have influenced the thinking in this piece. See Adriana Cavarero et al., *Diotima. Il pensiero della differenza sessuale* (Milan, 1987); the publications of the Libreria delle donne in Milan: 'Più donne che uomini', *Sottosopra*, January 1983; 'Sulla rappresentanza politica femminile', *Sottosopra*, June 1987; 'Un filo della felicità', *Sottosopra*, January 1989; Maria Luisa Boccia and Isabella Peretti (eds), 'Il genere della rappresentanza', supplement to *Democrazia e diritto*, no. 1, 1988. For an overview which gives an impression of the impact of the discussion on difference on a wide range of disciplines, see Maria Cristina Marcuzzo and Anna Rossi-Doria, *La ricerca delle donne. Studi femministi in Italia* (Turin, 1987).

8 The Early Socialist Critique of Democracy in Britain

Gregory Claeys

The rise of socialism after 1815 represents a watershed in the history of political thought.[1] Yet we do not, curiously, usually understand socialism as a particularly *political* movement. What was novel about socialism, instead, was its thoroughgoing critique of industrlialization, the division of labour and private property, its egalitarian economic and social relations, its communitarianism, and its feminism. Nonetheless political implications abound in these areas. Overshadowed by the canonization of Marx and Engels' works by the late nineteenth century, and the kidnapping of the entire socialist project by Marxism-Leninism, however, the origins of key elements in socialist political thought, such as its critique of democracy – clearly relevant to Marxism – remain shrouded.[2] This weakness in the intellectual history of socialism, moreover, hinders our capacity to comprehend why socialist politics have so often gone wrong, and why, particularly, the socialist critique of liberalism and radicalism has been often too complete, too unreflecting, and too uncritical of overly perfectionist alternatives.

Here I want briefly to explore how Owenite socialism in Britain created a distinctively new language of politics through a 'social' critique of the assumptions of both liberalism and Owenism's nearest competitor, the radical parliamentary reformers. The popularizing of this 'social' dimension had by 1850 effected a paradigmatic reconceptualization in radical politics whose implications remain on the whole unchanged, despite the failure of the more extreme forms of communism. Already evident by the mid-1820s were elements of the later socialist opposition to 'politics', of an ambiguity towards, if not outright opposition to, parliamentary institutions, and of the belief in the superiority of one 'party' (not always under this name), which came to define the politics of communist governments after 1917 and clearly facilitated tyrannical usurpation within such regimes. For such ideas socialism, through its subsequent inability to understand the virtues of political pluralism and toleration of minority rights, has thus paid an extraordinarily high price, not least in human life.

Yet what I will here term the 'perfectionist' or 'anti-political' ideal within socialism was only one, albeit the most unfortunate, outcome of the socialist critique of democracy. The roots of socialist opposition to both liberal and radical political thought lay in the accusation that both no longer suited the circumstances of the early nineteenth century. Many socialists believed that the outcome of the French Revolution, and particularly the emergence of the Terror and Napoleonic dictatorship, proved the failure of the politics of revolution generally, indeed of all schemes for quickly introducing universal suffrage. They insisted, moreover, that the revolution demonstrated the centrality of the subsistence question to any reform proposals, and after 1815 increasingly linked the question of feeding and employing the poor to industrial expansion. For socialists the centrality of 'economics' to 'politics' and the challenge posed to traditional radicalism by economic change was thus undoubted. It was over this issue, consequently, that the debate between liberalism and socialism came to define both nineteenth and twentieth century political thought, the key division between them lying in the question of the sufficiency of the universal formal political equality demanded by the new radicals of the 1790s in light of the greater social inequality and poverty of the post-Napoleonic period. Within socialism, the central political debate has undoubtedly been the relationship between the 'social' critique of democratic radicalism and the proposed politics of socialism itself, and whether 'liberal' institutions, mirroring the inequalities and competitiveness of commercial society, ought to be dispensed with, or whether a crotchety, burdensome parliamentary baby was better left soaking in somewhat murky bathwater – leaving its hands undoubtedly dirty – than ejected for the sake of scouring the tub. Yet there was not one, but a range of socialist responses to the problem of what sort of politics socialism could have, and my aim here is to examine both the political and anti-political, or perfectionist, strands in early socialism. To distinguish these we need firstly briefly to define the new forms of radicalism of the 1790s, which were the main target for the socialist attack upon 'politics', then to sketch the Owenite critique of democracy, outline its sources, and assess how these related to earlier forms of radical and republican thought.

Compared to the moderate Whiggism predominant throughout the eighteenth century, the new radicalism of the 1790s, identified in particular with Thomas Paine's extraordinarily influential *Rights of*

Man (1791–2), was much more democratic. Paine sought universal male suffrage, a written constitution along American lines, and representative institutions governing through an elected executive. Central to his political thought was the notion that inviolable natural rights served as the basis for all subsequent civil rights, and could be protected only by recognizing popular sovereignty and abolishing aristocratic and Anglican monopolies. Paine's vision was also rooted in a commercial optimism associated with the new United States, whose increasing opulence, he supposed, owed much to its form of government. 'Society', Paine thus assumed, was largely the product of interdependent needs which all sought to fulfill, and established its own order on the basis of mutual consent and interest. Paine hoped that when commerce had been universally extended, interdependence would unite all through the mutual satisfaction of wants, and warfare would cease after monarchies had been overthrown. This *laissez-faire* ideal was however tempered by welfare proposals, and a system of proportionate taxation reaching 100 per cent for landed estates worth more than £23 000 annually. Nor did Paine worry about political corruption through the extension of luxury, or fear, as many earlier republicans had done, that a modern division of labour made political participation by the ignorant majority impossible. He thus rejected the notion that fervent political virtue and commercial society were wholly incompatible, and that a widespread and deeply felt devotion to the common good was possible only in simple societies without substantial inequality (as republicans like Richard Price, William Godwin or Charles Hall believed).

In Britain the socialist critique of radicalism was begun by Robert Owen and his followers. Owen had become famous by managing the immensely successful cotton-spinning factory at New Lanark, which in his hands became renowned for creating a model, well-housed and reasonably paid but also disciplined and productive workforce. Deeply frustrated by his failure to extend this paternal, benevolent vision on a grander scale by achieving factory reforms, such as child labour laws, Owen by 1817 began to prophesy that industrialization by generating a small class of wealthy and a mass of poor threatened the entire fabric of society. Salvation from this impending fate, he proclaimed, would occur only if a 'new moral world' was created where all lived in 'co-operative communities' of about 2000 people, labouring and sharing property in common, combining agriculture and industry, rotating tasks, and superseding cities and indeed all existing social and political institutions. In an age of tremendous disruption this vision had considerable appeal, and between 1820 and 1850 Owen and his followers built about half a dozen communities in Britain and the US, of which the best-known were New Harmony in Indiana, and Harmony or Queenwood in Britain. In the mid-1830s Owen was involved in efforts to create one grand union of all labourers, and to generate direct exchanges of produce among the working classes, thus eliminating unnecessary retail trade. By the mid-1840s the British Owenite organization had some 10000 members; with the bankruptcy of Queenwood in 1845, however, the movement collapsed, and though Owen lived on until 1858 there was no substantial revival of socialism in Britain until the 1880s.

For all its lack of practical success, Owenism also generated an immense amount of printed literature, notably Owen's own voluminous works, but including well-known, detailed and sophisticated tracts like John Gray's *Lecture on Human Happiness* (1825), William Thompson's *Inquiry into the Principles of the Distribution of Wealth Most Conducive to Human Happiness* (1824), John Francis Bray's *Labour's Wrongs and Labour's Remedy* (1839), plus dozens of periodicals and hundreds of pamphlets. In their economic ideas such works largely defended the new communitarian ideal, sometimes from a more primitivist viewpoint, emphasizing the need to limit needs if distribution were to be equal and sufficient, but also (especially in the writings of Gray and Bray) increasingly urging the creation of what I have elsewhere termed 'economic socialism'. This took the nation-state rather than the community as the basic economic unit, and permitted the future expansion of both needs and productive capacity, while still defending labour's right to its produce and proposing the abolition of most of the 'unproductive classes'. Virtually all Owenite writers were agreed, however, that *laissez-faire* capitalism merely promised the greater degradation of the poor, and the generation of greater inequality through commercial crisis and the unjust reward of labour.

In its politics, which were intimately linked to these economic proposals, Owenism engaged in a deep and lengthy critique of the popular radical movement through the Chartist years, and first outlined virtually all of the later socialist and Marxist arguments against liberal democracy and 'mere' radical political reform. While most of Owen's followers accepted the gist of Owen's *critique* of democracy, and sought to found a new 'social science' (a term long synonymous with 'socialism') to replace traditional ideas of politics, many were nonetheless not prepared to entertain for long his more perfectionist assumptions about alternatives, and preferred more traditional solutions. The spectrum of Owenite political thought thus ranged from an 'anti-political' extreme embodied in Owen's own writings, on the one hand, to a new 'social democratic' alternative on the other.

The case many Owenites made against radical democratic theories of the sort associated with Paine can be grouped around the two sets of arguments, the economic and the political. The economic argument usually rested upon three premisses. Firstly, it was contended that the chief existing source of social disruption was mechanization. But while machinery now caused overproduction and unemployment, Owenites argued that it could help assure plenty for all, if just exchange and distribution and common ownership of the means of production were introduced. The radicals, they rightly insisted, said little about machinery, and certainly lacked the distinctly optimistic vision which Owen helped to popularize, and which was linked to the assumption that if machinery could help ensure opulence, many of the roots of existing social and political conflicts would be eliminated.

Secondly, the Owenites complained that while radicals continued to believe that the corrupt over-taxation of the working classes was the chief cause of distress, it could be proven that removing the value of the labourer's product by a process of unequal exchange (including labour for wages in the workplace), or giving the labourer less in return than his or her labour produced, amounted to a far greater sum than that removed via taxation. This emphasis upon the spheres of production and exchange, correspondingly, entailed focusing on men and women more as economic agents than citizens, and concentrating upon their rights as producers rather than as human beings (a view since proven dangerous to the protection of minority rights). Owen thus accepted the gist of the utilitarian attack on 'natural rights'. Consequently the central radical focus on natural civil and political rights was here largely displaced by a discourse on productivity which mirrored the emphasis though not the analyses and conclusions of classical political economy.

Thirdly, the vision that a commercial republic governed by popular consent through representative institutions would invariably diffuse opulence to all – the key economic promise of Paine's *Rights of Man* – seemed to the Owenites clearly disproven by the experience of the United States in the early decades of the nineteenth century. The equation of a republican form of government with high wages and relative prosperity may have been persuasive in the 1790s, assisted by limited information and the appeal of political novelty. By the 1830s, however, Owenites could point to increasing distress in the US, and this was central in convincing many of the need for socialism. (John Francis Bray, for example, was led to rewrite *Labour's Wrongs* completely by the astonishing realization that there were beggars in America too.) Socialists could thus now demonstrate

> the startling anomaly of a political constitution in America, framed on the principles of the radical politicians, co-existing with commercial embarrassment – a distressed labouring population and a continual struggle between the wealthy and poorer classes, as to who shall be master, and who the slave.[3]

These arguments collectively ensured that Owenites counselled the rejection of *laissez-faire* and argued for intervention and commercial regulation, though William Thompson and others did think some form of more egalitarian and just commerce might be compatible with some principles of free trade.

The second set of arguments used by British socialists against radicals concerned the inadequacies of existing and proposed representative, constitutional and democratic institutions. A common source of complaint was that the democratic process and parliamentary institutions were modelled upon and mirrored the competitive 'individualism' (a term first used in England by Owenite writers) of commercial society generally, and thus reflected and perpetuated divisive and hostile passions incompatible with any vision of harmonious association. Since they usually assumed that the Tory party embodied the landed, and the Whig the commercial, interest, the Owenites not infrequently derided parliament as merely reflecting the existing property system, or alternatively, as superfluous given the overwhelming power of economic factors in the formation of social policy, and the relative independence of the economy from political interference.

Thirdly, those socialists committed to community life could offer a further set of arguments about the inadequacies of existing political institutions by comparison with the virtues of 'community'. For many, indeed, the very prospect that the punitive and police powers of existing governments might be abolished – perhaps the most 'utopian' ideal, in the pejorative sense (there are others), ever incorporated into socialism, given the danger that it implied massive repression to make mankind so good – depended on all living in small groups rather than great cities and towns. The promise that community would supersede existing coercive forces hinged upon several related assumptions, but all of these rested upon an ideal of small group life; any notion that coercive restraint could be abolished in the wider nation-state (seemingly presumed in some later forms of socialism) was simply impossible on these premisses. Only in community could mutual supervision – the universalization of moral coercion in civil society – eliminate the need for many other police functions. Government by 'public opinion' would ensure moral conformity once the 'vicious' could no longer secrete themselves in the crowded alleys of great towns (Owen hoped to see grass growing over the streets of London). Only on such a small scale, too, could the education of the younger generation in Owenite principles reduce aggression generally, for the central principle of Owen's plans was the necessitarian assumption that character was formed by the environment, and that individuals correspondingly were not 'responsible' for much of their behaviour. Owen never articulated any very complex theory of the relationship between environment and character, and was unable to explain clearly how individuals might raise themselves above their 'circumstances' beyond merely following his instructions (a failing Marx took him to task for in the third 'Thesis on Feuerbach', though Marx's 'revolutionary practice' has not proven a more satisfactory answer as to how to educate the educators). But Owen took this theory to imply that once it was understood that blame could not be apportioned to individuals, all would treat others kindly and charitably. Such a demeanour of 'charity' was central to the 'new religion' Owen sometimes proposed to encompass his principles, but this was always a variation on secular notions of the determination of character.

As I indicated earlier, this critique of radicalism resulted in two main socialist political ideals, one of which, 'anti-political' socialism, is best associated with Owen himself, the other of which attempted to combine the assault on existing institutions with a new democratic form of socialism. Both of these however understood socialism as the extension of existing democratic practices, though for the anti-political perfectibilists this meant rejecting most existing forms of politics.

To those seeking one final, perfect form of association, then, 'true democracy' was impossible in commercial society, for the 'principle of individual interest' needed to be eliminated not only from economic life, but all institutions. To accomplish this Owen proposed replacing all existing modes of economic, social and political organization with a single communitarian model based upon the ideal family, and combining what Owen assumed were the best of both the aristocratic and democratic principles while eliminating conflicts of interest based on class and the division of labour. If the future society was organized around the principle of age instead of class, thought Owen, all would pass through the major occupations together, being educated, working as producers, supervising others, governing the community, and finally being responsible for relations between communities. This would ensure that no contest or struggle need determine who should govern. Existing democratic practices merely ensured conflict; elections called forth 'the worst feelings of our nature into constant action', by corrupting public morals, encouraging a lust for power, and dividing individuals.[4] If the labouring classes achieved power under the existing system, thought Owen, their behaviour would be no different than that of their masters, a prognosis he thought proven by the course of the French revolution. Owen's final plan thus proposed replacing all current institutions, including 'single family arrangements' (children would be educated in common), by eight age-groups. At ages 30–40 all would then govern the 'home department' of communities, and at 40–60, all 'foreign affairs'. Government would be by the 'paternal' or 'educational principle' of age, and not only would all contests for power cease, but the democratic premiss that all possessed the right to rule would be fulfilled as well, since all would eventually share in government. The new theory also eliminated the old republican problem of specialization, and the objection that a stultifyingly narrow division of labour rendered the working classes incapable of exercising their political rights virtuously. The notion that dependence was to be abolished was in this sense both central to the new perfectionist ideal, and a crucial link to older republican as well as Nonconformist ideas of independence (the most extreme of which verged upon antinomianism). In 1848 Owen thus wrote that in the future each would become 'his own priest, lawyer, physician and soldier, in order that each may be the most independent of others that social arrangements can be made to admit'.[5]

What were the sources of the perfectionist account of politics? Three traditions of political discourse entered prominently into Owen's ideal. The most important of these was republicanism, not, clearly, in its modern emphasis upon the value of constitutional balance, but in particular through its stress on the need for independent electors with adequate leisure to know the common good and act upon it, and sufficient wisdom to resist the temptations of luxury and vice, to avoid Court or government corruption through patronage, and to oppose standing armies. Owen and many of his followers also accepted the gist of the republican warning about the dangers of commercial society for public virtue, and of a narrow division of labour for both political responsibility and personal happiness (similar views were put forward by Charles Fourier in France). In some respects, indeed, socialism reverted to a more classical republican model of a small society in which the intensified love of the public good was possible (a devotion most eighteenth century writers agreed might have been a noble Greek and Roman ideal, but one impossible to implement in both large societies and commercial republics). Nonetheless Owenism also adopted a notion of independence considerably different from that of most republicans, and much closer, indeed, in its unity of social roles, to the critique of the division of labour and pursuit of 'all-rounded development' (uniting, for example, hunting, fishing and critical criticism) which we associate with Marx's *German Ideology*. Owenism also accepted a Quaker insistence upon the need to eliminate war entirely (though Owen was not averse in the interim to communities training their members as militias for self-defence). Rejecting the usual republican focus upon the nation, and crucially deriding patriotism – the central republican ideal – as the highest form of good, moreover, socialism dismissed national chauvinism and urged universal benevolence, with Owen taking this principle to the extreme, urging the abolition of all national boundaries and linguistic differences and the creation of a broad uniformity to ensure that no further sources of conflict existed (he later protested that he did not seek to eradicate individual differences). Most Owenites were probably unwilling to go so far, but nonetheless accepted the thesis that the division of labour, and not merely the existence of a system of private property, was a central element in the degradation of the poor and the competition of interests in society.

A second major component in the perfectionist account of politics was radical puritanism, and especially Quakerism. The Quakers had of course long been renowned for their principled pacifism and stubborn egalitarian unwillingness to compromise with the established order. Politically they particularly interested Owen because conflict in their sect was adjudicated without elections or voting, by emphasizing consensus and achieving harmony wherever possible through unanimity, with government within the sect being broadly through the rule of wise elders. What Owen here shared with Quakerism was an abhorrence of 'politics' as an unnatural activity to be everywhere avoided. This was derived in part from a Manichaean dualism markedly present in Christian thought from Augustine onwards, which produced a sharp distinction between a corrupt 'City of Man' and an ideal unity of Christian believers in the City of God which could be read in terms of an antinomy of 'politics' and 'harmony'. For Owen this was also united with a quasi-millennarian language which strongly contrasted the virtues of the 'new moral world' with the vices of its imperfect predecessor.

Finally, the idea that 'politics' might somehow be superseded in socialism was also indebted to a variety of accounts of primitive society, the golden age and the state of nature, and the assumption that 'natural man' was essentially sociable and harmoniously organized, and was only divided by artificial institutions. Here a clear debt to the leading 'sociability' theorists of the eighteenth century (like Shaftesbury and Rousseau) was evident, as was a strong if qualified admiration for the North American natives in particular.

Most socialists shared in these assumptions to a degree, but for many, indeed the vast majority of Owen's working class followers, such objections to the inadequacies of present political institutions pointed not towards the need to supersede them by creating a perfect ideal, of which many were sceptical, but to extend democracy further and remove its existing class basis and biases. Those Owenites who attempted to combine socialism and democracy – many in the 1840s were also Chartists – accepted the parliamentary struggle, the need for elections, the ballot, and replaceable public officials, and also the principle of specialization generally, if not its more extreme forms. They largely agreed, however, that the Owenite analysis of society had invalidated many older radical assumptions, conceding the importance of machinery and exchange in relation to taxation, and admitting growing distress in America. Consequently their main concern was to recraft the older radicalism in order to satisfy the new social critique. By the late 1840s, thus, a new group of social radicals had begun to emerge, through such organizations as the British Association for the Promotion of Co-operative Knowledge and the National Union of the Working Classes, who wedded Owenite and radical aims in various mixtures. During the Chartist years such views were combined by some of the 'moral force' Chartists around William Lovett, the 'Chartist Socialists' led by James Napier Bailey, and by the Chartist leader James Bronterre O'Brien (marginalized through much of the 1840s by Feargus O'Connor). The social radicals termed themselves 'social and political reformers' to indicate that *political* means were to be used to secure *social* ends (which might or might not be 'socialist'). 'Politics' thus remained a legitimate vehicle for gaining reforms, but the aims of reform were no longer construed as freeing the economy from governmental interference or overly heavy taxation, but rather in terms of establishing co-operatives or communities, relieving the poor, regulating wages and similar measures. Universal suffrage was thus no longer viewed as being mechanically a guarantee of working class opulence. A more complex theory of the relationship of economics to politics had emerged.

Although the organized Owenite movement continued to concentrate upon founding a model community, many socialists by the late 1840s had come to believe that the nation-state was the appropriate sphere and focus of socialist activity, regardless of what role communities might play within the state. It was thus widely assumed that some institutions of centralized direction and administration would probably remain in the future, and also that new, more democratic intermediary institutions might be created. By this time, moreover, those social radicals who accepted something of Owen's plans (like O'Brien, here largely following John Gray) also tended to opt for co-operative industrial proposals and reward according to labour, rather than a complete community of goods and equal remuneration. 'Political socialism' in this sense tended to be correlated to 'economic socialism', or the willingness to accept expanding needs and productive capacity rather than a more frugal vision of communitarian autarky and full communism. With this compromise came the additional acknowledgement that the nearly complete abolition of the traditional conception of the division of labour proposed by Owen was impossible, if not also undesirable, some specialization being necessary to increasing returns and more universal opulence. The vision of social complexity entailed here also implied a much higher level of political activity than Owen himself sought for the future. In this regard, however, the creation of democratic socialism also involved the *extension* of traditional democratic practices beyond the parliamentary sphere and into, in particular, the economy. For John Francis Bray, for example, it was essential to have elected regulatory boards to supervise production and distribution, while in the quasi-syndicalist schemes of Owen's chief lieutenant during the early 1830s, James Elishama Smith, trades would oversee the productive process. In many such proposals, moreover, frequent rotation was emphasized as an important aspect of ensuring that political control did not become professionalized or ossified bureaucratically, and as a means of ensuring working class control over the economy.

Early British socialism thus produced a spectrum of views on political activity ranging from the anti-political notions of Owen himself to new forms of socialist democracy. By implying that there is a socialist discourse on politics shared by early socialism as well as Marxism, a reconstruction of these ideas clarifies the historical origins of the propensity of later communist parties to aim at 'harmonious' rule excluding competition from other parties or factions, in practice opting for that government by age (albeit often by geriatric party members well beyond Owen's age limits) which Owen thought best avoided political conflict. Nonetheless it also shows us that an overriding desire for perfect 'harmony' is not endemic to socialism, but only its least sceptical varieties. Secondly, such a reconstruction throws into considerable doubt the dominant organizing scheme for discussing the evolution of socialism in the nineteenth century, namely the transition from the 'utopian' socialism of Owen, Fourier, Saint-Simon and others to the 'scientific' socialism of Marx and Engels. Far more of what was later termed 'scientific socialism' was in fact already in evidence in the early years of the socialist movement than this overly-sharp distinction implies. In particular, Engels was wrong (in his famous *Socialism: Utopian and Scientific*) to see all forms of early socialism as (1) bound to the assumption that the proletariat was merely a 'suffering mass', since the political socialists indeed accepted an active role for the working class; as (2) insistent in the view that society could only be transformed by propaganda and experiments, when parliamentary reform was indeed the primary means chosen by the more political socialists; and (3) refusing to believe that the seeds of the new society lay in the economic development of the old, and that socialism could be founded at any time or place in history, when even Owen himself insisted that socialism was possible only after the industrial age had arrived, and most Owenites accepted some version of the well-known four-stages theory of history (in variants not so different from that which appears in the *German Ideology*). Some periodization of 'early' to 'later' socialism is of course still desirable, and there remain crucial differences between Owenism, Fourierism, the views of Weitling and so on, and those of Marx and Engels. But a number of vital theoretical transitions did occur *within* early socialism – indeed in Britain often in reaction to Owen's own views, and his attempt to impose these on others – rather than after it, amongst them the emergence of many socialist views of politics prominent in later decades. Some of the new views of politics, we have seen, were tied to older but now reconstituted notions of republican and Nonconformist 'independence'; in other respects, for example in the idea of electing working class representatives to supervise production, there were few parallels to the past. In both cases there was a decidedly richer and more complex conception of politics than has been hitherto assumed. The perfectionist variant of this approach to liberal politics is not thoroughly bankrupt. But if illiberal communism is dead, many varieties of social democracy, evident for example in some schemes of co-ownership or co-operation, as well as many other forms of political institution, have yet to be widely tested, and continue to promise greater participation, autonomy and collective control than existing mechanisms provide.

NOTES

1. This chapter outlines and extends some of the arguments of my *Citizens and Saints. Politics and Anti-Politics in Early British Socialism* (Cambridge: Cambridge University Press, 1989).
2. A recent exception is Keith Taylor, *The Political Ideals of the Utopian Socialists* (London: Frank Cass, 1982). There are also useful comments in Vincent Geoghegan, *Utopianism and Marxism* (London: Methuen, 1987).
3. *New Moral World*, 4, no. 161 (25 November 1837), p. 37.
4. Robert Owen, *Public Discussion between Robert Owen and the Rev. J. H. Roebuck* (1837), p. 115.
5. *The Spirit of the Age*, no. 16 (16 November 1848), p. 244.

9 British Socialism and Democracy in Retrospect

Fred Whitemore

The crisis of socialism in the 1980s has had at its centre the question of democracy. While this has been most acutely experienced in the communist regimes of Eastern Europe and China, there have been loud and certainly politically significant echoes of the same problems in Britain and other Western countries where reformist or social democratic versions of socialism have played a major role in creating the economic and political systems of the post-war world.

Put simply, the issue has been that the methods and structures, created to deal with the social and industrial problems which socialists helped make the focus of political attention, have been experienced as profoundly alien by the people they were designed to benefit. To make matters worse, in Britain socialists and Labour governments were often primarily responsible for the creation and adoption of those methods and structures. As Doreen Massey, Lynne Segal and Hilary Wainwright, writing in 1983, put it, 'nationalised industries are unresponsive to both worker and consumer. On a day to day level many people do experience the welfare state as undemocratic, impenetrable and even hostile'.[1]

Added to the bureaucratic administration of agencies and services without any real feeling of democratic control or accountability has been a process of centralization and concentration of political control. In part this has taken the form of the erosion of the independence and responsibilities of local government. And Governments of the Left have played a full part in that process. It was, for example, the nationalization measures of the post-war Labour Government which removed from local control the running of gas, water and electricity in areas where these, and sometimes other services, had been municipalized. The Morrisonian model of national administration of these industries represented much less obvious and direct political supervision than had existed at the local level.

Again, where at the beginning of the century – in the case of education and welfare provision through the poor law – separately elected bodies existed at the local level for the administration of services, these were first incorporated into the role of the single local government authority, and then directly or indirectly made increasingly subject to national control. Here, too, the Left, or sections of the Left, welcomed, and after 1945 was in part responsible for, the change. There was certainly no marked tendency to resist, and no attempt to reverse these developments. So this process, which constituted part of what Colin Leys has labelled 'de-democratization',[2] was one in which the British Left was firmly implicated, and for which it was arguably mainly responsible.

During the 1960s, 1970s and 1980s resentment about what had occurred grew and became a matter of concern and debate across the political spectrum. Why this should have happened at that time is not difficult to understand but can perhaps be illustrated simply through one example – the provision of local authority housing. In the 1930s, late 1940s and early 1950s those who acquired council houses experienced the change as a liberation from the conditions of the slums and the pressures of acute post-war housing shortage. It hardly seemed to matter that the relationship with the officials who administered housing was little different from that with a private landlord; nor that these officials increasingly made the decisions about housing management, as the growth of housing provision itself in practice limited any effective detailed democratic control by elected Councillors. To the next generation, who took the existence of a reasonable standard of housing for granted, the way housing was run became central. Its administration appeared increasingly unresponsive or indifferent to the wishes and needs of tenants, while the local Council and Councillors seemed to offer no route by which officialdom could be effectively influenced or controlled.

This example could, in essence, be replicated across the range of services which national and local government had come to provide. The problem was recognized by both Left and Right. But it was to be the political Right which benefited decisively from it, with a philosophy which suggested that the root of the difficulty lay in state provision itself, and that the solution was to be found in a new or revamped role for market forces. The triumph of the Right in this respect reflected the fact that it proved more effective in translating a theoretical response into a rage of policies taken up by a political party and offered to the electorate. But it was also a product of the fact that the Left was seen to be mainly responsible for the situation, and that socialism had come to be perceived as commitment to the bureaucratic and centralized state.

If the Left had earlier developed a set of practices to achieve a more equal distribution of power, and real participation in decision-making, to accompany the measures through which it had sought greater social and economic equality, it might have been easier to counter the promise of freedom and control which the Right offered through personal ownership and the market. Part of the problem of the British Left in the 1980s was, therefore, not only its identification with a bureaucratic system, but that it now paid a heavy political price for that identification. It was to suffer the humiliation of seeing those for whose benefit it believed it had introduced reforms, apparently indifferent to, or even supportive of, the dismantling of such reforms.

The object of this chapter is to explore how the British Left came to find itself in this position. It will be argued that it did so because it almost always failed to take the question of democracy sufficiently seriously. Above all it had failed to formulate either a theory or a proposed system of democracy to match the institutional developments which arose from its social and economic concerns and policies.

On the surface, the failure of the British Left during the past century in this respect is surprising. Most British socialists would have proclaimed themselves passionate adherents of a democratic creed. Those who in the 1880s gravitated towards socialism and created the foundations of the British socialist movement came mainly from extreme radical democratic politics. Again and again British socialists, and then the Labour party, were to trumpet the claimed superiority of their commitment to democracy over that of their political rivals. One example will suffice: in 1918 the Labour Party's policy document 'Labour and the New Social Order' proclaimed 'what marks off this Party most distinctively from any of the other political parties is its demand for the full and genuine adoption of the principle of democracy'.[3] Already by 1918, however, it was clear that this commitment, no matter how seriously held, meant little in terms of concrete policies. Certainly it was not matched by proposals in any way comparable to those which gave the Party's social and economic aspirations their meaning.

BEFORE 1914

A number of related factors in the theory and the practice of British socialism over the thirty or so years before 1914 explain this fact.

In the early years of British socialism, especially on the left of the movement, democracy was understood more as a sentiment than as a system of institutional arrangements. This is nowhere clearer than in Edward Carpenter's *Towards Democracy*. *Towards Democracy* was written in 1882 as Carpenter's ideas were becoming more socialist. The book significantly influenced the perceptions of many early socialists, especially those within what has come to be known as the 'ethical socialist' tradition. But as Carpenter said in a letter to Walt Whitman, whose own work had inspired the book, 'I have thought for some time of calling it Towards Democracy and I do not see any reason for altering the title – though the word Democracy does not often occur in it'.[4] Where the word did occur, it was clear that democracy was to be understood primarily as a sentiment colouring all other aspects of existence. In the short prose poem on 'The Word Democracy' Carpenter wrote

> Underneath all now comes this Word, turning the edges of the other words where they meet it.
>
> Politics, art, science, commerce, religion, customs and methods of daily life, the very outer shows and semblances or ordinary objects . . .
>
> . . . Their meanings must all now be absorbed and recast in this word, or else fall off like dry husks before its disclosure.[5]

Where democracy meant anything more precise, the word had the meaning common before the definite development of Liberal Democratic theory: the assertion of the power of the lower orders, and the destruction of that of the establishment. As Carpenter writes, 'Democracy just begins to open her eyes and peep! and the rabble of unfaithful bishops, priests, generals, landlords, capitalists, lawyers, kings, queens, patronisers and polite idlers goes scuttling down into general oblivion'.[6]

On some parts of the Left democracy continued to be understood in these general, vague and perhaps utopian terms. On other parts of the Left vagueness about it was turned into a virtue, precisely to avoid the charge of utopianism. As William Morris put it, 'We Socialists are satisfied with demanding what we think necessary for [the new] Society to form itself – this we think better than putting forward elaborate utopian schemes for the future'.[7] And when, in *News From Nowhere*, Morris was tempted into describing in some detail the character of British socialist society, projected around two hundred years into the future, the question of government still remained vague. We are told by the guide to the new world, with some precision, that the old Parliament has become a dung-market, but on the positive side only 'that our present parliament would be hard to house in one place, because the whole people is our parliament'.[8] When the question of decision-making is raised, it becomes clear that there are units of government – 'a commune, or a ward, or a parish' – and that meetings of neighbours takes place.[9] But the example of a decision which Morris gives – characteristically the replacement of an ugly old iron bridge by a new stone one – is of a simple low-level nature.[10] There is nothing which even begins to constitute a clear picture of government (or, as Morris would prefer to call it, management) and decision-making in the new society.

This tendency to remain vague about the character of future democracy, either to convey its ethereal quality, or to avoid the charge of utopian speculation, was reinforced by a third factor, which was especially evident among those most influenced by Marxism. The essential task of socialism, Marxists held, was a transformation of the economic system which would take power from the capital owning class. This transformation would put power in the hands of the working class. It was assumed that the political form in which such power would be exercised was democracy. Indeed the economic transformation was seen as both a necessary and sufficient condition for the achievement of true democracy. One might therefore make demands for democratic reforms under capitalism (although without much hope of any great success); but to concern oneself with the form of democracy under socialism was quite inappropriate and even a distraction.

The view that the principal work of socialists must be to achieve change in the economic and social sphere was mirrored on the right of British socialism. This after all, it was assumed, was what socialism was really about, and what distinguished it from liberalism. Socialists might therefore support every democratic reform, and even want to go further and faster than liberalism, but this was not a matter that should be the central focus of socialist thinking or work. Socialists must bring to the top of the political agenda questions of poverty, low wages, unemployment, poor housing, bad health, oppressive industrial relations. On questions of purely political reform they should play a subsidiary, if supportive, role.

This attitude was expressed most overtly in the writings of Ramsay MacDonald. MacDonald believed that society and history progressed through a series of evolutionary stages. The current stage was the

Economic Stage. From that would emerge the Moral Stage when, as he claimed in his first major work, *Socialism and Society*, published in 1905, socialism 'springs into life'.[11] It was, however, during the existing 'Economic Stage' that the democratic state developed. And that development he says (and notice the past tense) 'has been the chief contribution of Liberalism to the evolution of social functions and their organisation'.[12] Liberalism, he maintains, 'stood in the political sphere for enfranchisement, for freedom, for democracy', although he concedes 'its battles have not been won fully' and 'the finishing touches will not be put upon political democracy until the existing constitution is proved to be a barrier to social legislation'.[13]

In writing this MacDonald had a clear political objective. Liberalism (and hence the Liberal Party) was to be seen as part of a past, or at least passing, era. Socialism (and hence the Labour Party) represented the future. Democracy had been, or had almost been, achieved. Socialism could simply build on that, providing no more than 'the finishing touches' to it.

Strange as this view may seem in a period when only around two-thirds of adult males had the vote and the House of Lords retained all its old formal powers, it was the view of most moderate British Socialists, and indeed was a view reinforced in them through MacDonald's avowal of it. By 1914 therefore, although these socialists might care deeply about certain specific issues, such as the House of Lords or the enfranchisement of women, they (or most of them) had come to accept the broad framework of British parliamentary representative democracy as constituting democracy itself, and as being a political framework within which and from which socialism could be achieved. In doing this they had also come to accept a very much narrower view of democracy than would have seemed appropriate to nearly all socialists a generation earlier – even though, as we have seen, those earlier socialists failed to make concrete or clear the form or structure of democracy which they desired. Any feeling that there might be a need to modify the institutions and procedures of representative democracy to match projected changes in the economic and social structure of society was abandoned. Ideas for a wider and more direct or participatory form of democracy – earlier seen, at least implicitly, as part of socialist transformation – were dropped.

While the implications of this substantial contraction of the meaning of democracy was hardly understood by many British socialists, in one important section of the movement it was broadly welcome.

It is always difficult to generalize about the attitude of the Fabians. Fabianism has rightly and frequently been described as an eclectic doctrine. Different Fabians might well hold substantially different views. But if there was in any sense a core of orthodox Fabianism, it was, certainly in this period, to be found in the ideas of the Webbs.

In 1896 Sidney Webb had turned his mind to the question of democracy and delivered six lectures on the subject. In these lectures Webb rejected all specific schemes then under discussion for a form of democracy other than that of a strictly limited representative character. The mass meeting, the initiative, the referendum were all ruled out as methods of decision-making. Legislation, he argued, 'is as much a distinct craft as that of shoemaking'. Making law was a matter for the expert: electors might know the problems, but they would certainly not know how to solve them. Representatives should teach as well as learn. Democracy was desirable and had a role, but it was a restricted one. It was needed to prevent the potential misuse of their role by the expert legislators, but the most that could be allowed to, or expected of, democracy was the ratification or rejection of well-prepared schemes.[14]

This was no more than 'protective Democracy'.[15] It was designed to ensure that while the power to formulate and direct remained with the (preferably trained) expert (a central preoccupation of the Webbs and perhaps of Fabians more generally), a mechanism would exist to prevent those experts abusing power.

Webb's bureaucratic/democratic utopia had not, of course, been reached by 1914. But his influential view fitted fairly comfortably with the decline in expectations of democracy and the range of its operation which, for other reasons, had become the mood of the mainstream of British socialism at that date.

THE PERIOD OF RADICAL CHALLENGE

This mood was soon, however, to experience challenge and disruption. The period towards the end of the First World War, and the two years which followed, arguably constituted the period of greatest radical rethinking amongst British socialists. The war itself, the impact of the Russian revolution, the mood of confidence generated by a decade of rapid growth in trade unionism and Labour electoral support, all pushed in the direction of a reappraisal and widening of purpose. This was the period in which Clause 4.4 of the Labour

Party's constitution was adopted with minimal controversy, and even Webb in *Labour and the New Social Order* could accept that in some sense the extension of democracy to industry was needed.

In 1915 a section of the Fabians had broken away from the main society to form the National Guilds League, an organization which was to have as members some of the outstanding intellectuals of the period (including Bertrand Russell) and some of those who were to become most influential in British socialist thinking in the interwar years (including R. H. Tawney and Harold Laski).

Guild Socialism was in part a concession and in part a response to the claims of Syndicalism from those who broadly held more conventional views of the process of transition to socialism and the general nature of socialist politics. Now, in one of its leading members, G. D. H. Cole, it provided a theorist who would make the only substantial attempt in the history of British socialist thought to formulate a system of democracy which neither, on the one hand, accepted what was rapidly becoming the Marxist view of socialism and democracy, nor, on the other, simply accommodated to the theory and practice of Liberal Democracy to date.

In *Guild Socialism Restated*, published in 1920, Cole saw the weakness of mainstream British socialism as the drive to 'the completion of the present tendency towards State Sovereignty, by the piling of fresh powers and duties on the great Leviathan'.[16] This could never produce a true democracy which required the application of democratic action to specific purpose or function in society. For that, decision-making must be decentralized and must involve 'an active not merely a passive citizenship'.[17] It was only such democracy, he asserted, that 'can hope to call out the best in its members, or to give that maximum opportunity for personal and social self-expression which is requisite to real freedom'.[18] But if such democracy were achieved it would lead to 'an immense liberation of social and individual energy'.[19]

Cole's view of democracy was therefore of a participatory and developmental character. The bulk of *Guild Socialism Restated* consisted of the elaboration of the complex system needed to produce it. Cole began with, and put great stress on, the democracies of producers, developing out of trade unionism. But his system included democracies of consumers, professional services, citizens' organizations, as well as communes at a local, regional and national level. The complexities of these bodies, their powers and inter-relationships, is daunting, and one sometimes feels that if other socialists had failed to be precise about their understanding of a democratic system, Cole was over-compensating. But at least this achieved the objective of showing that a demand for a different form of democracy need not be mere words. It gave substance to the view that the economic and social measures associated with socialism could and should lead to a strengthening, not a weakening, of democratic control.

The impact of Cole's conceptions was such that even the Webbs felt they must respond. Their *A Constitution for the Socialist Commonwealth of Great Britain* (the publication of which slightly predated Cole's *Guild Socialism Restated* – although not of course the currency of its ideas) is often seen to represent major concessions on their part to Cole's position. And in some ways it does. There is generous tribute to, and apparent acceptance of, Cole's case for functional representation. There is an assertion of the need to apply democracy in industries and services, as well as emphasis on the role of democracy in the development of personality. In their central point – the need for a second or Social Parliament, in addition to the one dealing with more traditional matters – there is a significant practical shift towards Cole's view.

But the Webbs soon draw the line in terms of both the form of control this Parliament is to exercise, and in the extent of control of management from below. 'It must be made clear', they insist, 'that there is no idea of the Social Parliament . . . itself undertaking the complicated work of the administration of the socialized industries and services'.[20] Nor would employees appoint or dismiss managers. Any claim that they should do so was based on 'a primitive and indeed obsolete conception of democracy'.[21] Managers must be the best people qualified for the position and the way to obtain such people is through selection committees and appointments boards. The older view again comes through: the real business of administration is for those expert in it. Democracy, although now somewhat wider and organized somewhat differently, is still of the protective variety.

All this might have been the beginning of an interesting debate. But what could have become a new departure in thinking about socialism and democracy remained largely an incident in British socialist thought. Guild Socialism and with it Cole's application of it to political structures was killed, not by intellectual defeat, but by economic circumstances. Guild Socialist sentiment had been in part a product of the trade union boom in the decade from 1910. It had fed on the growing strength and numbers, the widening influence, and the increasing self-confidence of that movement. Now, in the early 1920s, as the economic depression came on trade unionism was weakened and declined, just as it was to be in the similar circumstances of the early 1980s. A severe blow was the collapse of the National Builders Guild in 1922. With all this Guild Socialism lost its impetus and its influence.

THE INTER-WAR YEARS

Echoes of this debate on democracy can be found in the thinking of some socialist theorists – particularly in Laski – during the 1920s. But broadly British reformist socialism and especially the Labour Party resumed its unquestioning acceptance of the already established political system as an adequate vehicle for socialism. Indeed its commitment to it was strengthened, firstly as some of those 'finishing touches' to which MacDonald had referred – especially votes for women – were provided, and secondly as the Labour Party itself proved increasingly successful within the Parliamentary system. During the 1920s interest in and support for even limited reforms such as proportional representation perceptibly declined. Demand for the abolition of the House of Lords became mainly a matter of ritual incantation, not a serious matter on the political agenda.

Once more this mood was to be disturbed, this time by the political crisis of 1931. The disintegration and collapse of the Labour Government in the summer of that year, in the face of economic problems and pressures, suggested strongly to those on the left of the Labour Party that what British communists had been asserting since 1920 might be broadly correct: British liberal parliamentary representative democracy merely masked the power of capital, national and international. That power would never permit a transition to socialism through the parliamentary system, nor even the concession of significant socialist measures of reform.

The rise of Communism had created a sharp difference between British socialists over the assessment of existing democratic forms. Before the First World War there had not, in practice, been any Chinese wall between most revolutionary or Marxist socialists on the one hand, and reformist socialists on the other, over the question of the use of Parliament (William Morris had been a rare exception in his absolute rejection of it). It was very much more, at least until the rise of Syndicalism, a question of emphasis in the significance attached to work centred on Parliament. Now, influenced by Leninism, a whole section of the Left condemned such work except for propagandist or strictly tactical purposes. During the 1920s the principal consequence of this was to limit the influence of communists outside their own party and front organizations. The experience of 1931 created sympathy for their perspective among a wider socialist audience. This was particularly reflected in the writing of Harold Laski, although he never fully committed himself to their view of the matter.

While this response was mainly concerned with the questioning of 'capitalist democracy' as an effective means for achieving socialism, it also again, though briefly, generated interest in alternative forms of democracy. This was especially marked within the Socialist League, the successor to the now disaffiliated ILP inside the Labour Party, where the influence of former Guild Socialists was initially strong.

The impact of 1931 was soon however eclipsed by questions of much wider import. By the late 1930s British socialism was clearly returning to its acceptance of existing constitutional arrangements. A major factor in this change was the rise of Fascism. Capitalist democracy, even if it was *capitalist* democracy, was worth defending and might need to be defended. If you were prepared to defend it in arms, was it not at least psychologically necessary to defend it in principle?

A more subtle influence was the changing perception of Soviet Communism. The trials and purges of the late 1930s, with an increasing awareness of comparisons between Fascist rule and Stalinism, brought a jolt to many socialists who had previously felt a degree of sympathy for the Soviet regime. One important consequence was to discredit the view that there could be a form of democracy which rejected the capitalist democracy of the West in favour of a more genuine, more socialist democratic system. That view had been principally held and advocated by communists since the First World War. But they were the strictest defenders of the Russian regime and often suggested that the Soviet system *was* the higher form of democracy already in operation. Was not the claim of a better alternative simply a fraud and deceit? On this basis many socialists came to see the *general* claim that a more socialist democratic alternative existed as an example of what might later have been called 'newspeak': tyranny was freedom; bureaucratic authoritianism was true democracy. These feelings were expressed strongly in the writings of British Socialists of the late 1930s. In 1938 R. H. Tawney added a chapter on 'Socialism and Democracy' to his book *Equality*. Tawney did not present western political systems as unblemished. In western society democracy with inequalities of wealth and power created 'an unstable compound'.[22] The principles of liberty, equality before the law, and political democracy, though undisputed, were 'confronted by an array of hostile powers, which ... prevent their application'.[23] Despite all this, political democracy did exist and socialists must accept two things: first, that given a choice between capitalist democracy and undemocratic socialism, the working class would always choose the former; and second, as he put it, 'given the existence of political democracy . . . the only possible course for socialists is to take the rough with the smooth'.[24] In other words, and with all the qualifications, the existing system of democracy must be accepted.

This conclusion was spelt out even more bluntly in a work of major influence published two years later. Evan Durbin's *The Politics of Democratic Socialism* is widely seen as the precursor of the 'new right' socialism which came to prominence in the 1950s, mainly associated with the writings of Tony Crosland and the leadership of Hugh Gaitskell. Durbin was clear and explicit about his endorsement of the existing system. 'The type of democracy that we enjoy', he argued, is 'the only type of democracy in the least applicable to the immense aggregates of population composing the modern nation state.'[25] Socialists must accept that adherence to it 'is an essential principle' and that socialism 'cannot be separated from it'.[26] He is scathing about the view that true democracy could only come with an end of social inequalities and economic insecurity. 'Utopia', he says, 'by any other name will smell as sweet and look as remote.'[27] In these circumstances the first and principle duty of socialists must be to defend existing democracy. All else if necessary must be sacrificed to it. Adherence to that principle required 'that we should be pacific and believe in compromise'.[28] Consequently a Labour Party programme, while needing to command support in the reforming party, must above all avoid driving the opposition to armed resistance.[29] As for such ideas as 'workers' control', the most they must be allowed to mean was limited workers' representation on the boards of nationalized industries. But control must be exercised in the interests of the community, not of the workers employed in the industries.[30] And that meant it must be exercised through the existing institutions of democracy.

Thus, while the thrust of the argument was to resist a view that social change might legitimately require or use means which compromised established democratic methods, it had a further consequence: the positive commitment to democracy as exemplified by current practice was taken to exclude any radical development or extension of democracy, or any reconsideration of the way a more complete democratic control might be organized.

THE CLIMAX OF SOCIALIST INFLUENCE

During the 1940s the tendency of British socialists simply to underwrite the existing British political system was reinforced by other factors.

Although, as we have seen, the response of most British socialists to the rise of Fascism was an intensified commitment to the existing democratic system, some on the left of the movement reacted differently. They were convinced that liberal representative institutions were simply adopted as a convenience by the ruling class. That class would, in Britain as elsewhere, if necessary or as appropriate throw them over for Fascism. Certainly the establishment would not go out of its way to defend them.

While a few could retain this view in the face of British participation in war against Fascism – the war they held was a fight for British imperial interests not for a system of government – most abandoned it. The change was strongly reinforced by the more obvious commitment to a fight to the finish against the Fascist powers after May 1940, linked to the participation of the Labour Party in a coalition dedicated to that course. The willingness of the British government from the summer of 1941 to work closely with Soviet Russia to defeat Fascism cemented this feeling, especially amongst those previously attracted to the Communist perspective. Parliamentary democracy came to be seen by many on the Left, who previously viewed it with profound suspicion, as something genuine and solid. It was not just a cover for the interests of their class enemies.

This more positive perception of the system was strengthened by the experience of the 1945 Labour Government. The election of that Government and its ability to carry through in broad terms the programme on which it was elected undermined the sentiment generated by 1931. There was no sabotage of either a flagrant or subtle character. Socialist advance might not be as fast as many desired, but clearly it was possible within the existing political framework.

Trust in and respect for established democratic institutions increasingly characterized the attitude of the Left. Only marginal reforms – the abolition of the business vote, the elimination of university representation, a further reduction in the power of the Lords – were seen as necessary. The idea that radical political reform to achieve a wider, more participatory, system of control matching the changes in social and economic policy and management, weak or imprecise as that commitment had usually been in the past, was now almost entirely lost. This can be seen very clearly in the writings of those on the left and the right of the Labour Party by the 1950s.

In his statement of personal creed *In Place of Fear*, published in 1952, Nye Bevan expresses it perfectly. Democracy he claims is still young in Britain – he dates it from 1929 – and hence its potential is as yet unfulfilled. But it is in essence 'a sword pointed at the heart of property power'. Bevan knows that Parliament can be 'profoundly intimidating for the products of a Board School system who are the bearers of a fiery message'. He concedes that it is consequently 'a shock absorber placed between privilege and the pressure of popular discontent'. Yet his answer to this problem is not institutional change but 'a big lump of irreverence'.[31] Bevan acknowledges too that 'much more is needed if the vast state apparatus is to be brought under control'.[32] But this crucial qualification which might have generated a wide rethinking of the process of democratic management and control leads him only to demand better clerical and office facilities for MPs. Even the recognition that the boards of the nationalized industries are 'a constitutional outrage' and that 'we have still to ensure thay are taking us towards Democratic Socialism' leads him only to demand accountability to a Minister, and vaguely that 'workers in the nationalized sector are made aware of a changed relationship between themselves and the management'.[33] In practice therefore Bevan accepts that existing arrangements, with no more than a slight adjustment of attitudes and practices, provide all that is necessary and sufficient for a socialist system.

Acceptance of the political status quo was still greater on the Labour right, even among the strongly emerging 'radical' right of the Party. Tony Crosland's *The Future of Socialism* contained no substantial analysis of, indeed hardly a reference to, questions of the form or organization of democracy. It is largely taken for granted that what is needed in this respect has already been achieved. There is, however, the odd side-swipe at those who may think otherwise. In a brief review of past socialist ideas Crosland dismisses advocates of workers' control, Syndicalists and Guild Socialists, for starting with an analysis of the oppressed condition of workers which 'clearly makes no sense today'.[34] In the context of a discussion of good industrial relations he argues, 'it is not easy to avoid a certain irritation when one hears the word "participation"', and 'we surely do not want a world in which everyone is fussing around in an interfering and responsible manner'.[35]

At the point where the Labour Party was to make its most decisive direct impact on British institutions, the 1940s, it had also most accommodated to the form of democracy already practised in Britain. Consideration of different or radical forms of democracy was at its minimum. The democracy which was endorsed was C. B. Macpherson's 'pluralist élitist equilibrium' model. The role of the populace was merely to choose between competing groups of politicians who, through winning elections, were empowered to decide policy.

This commitment arose primarily from the specific influences of the period. Not only were socialists reconciled to the political system for the reasons examined. Their priority was also to achieve a system of planning which would overcome the perceived failings of capitalism, especially unemployment, and later it was hoped achieve sustained high levels of economic growth. Such planning suggested bureaucratic and centralized management and made wider democratic participation seem irrelevant or even counter-productive.

But neglect, in this crucial era, of concern for institutional reform to strengthen democracy was also facilitated by the low level of attention this question had traditionally received. Consequently Cole's warning about 'the piling of fresh powers and duties on the great Leviathan' was ignored at precisely the point British socialism might most readily have avoided or mitigated the danger. In this respect the record of the post-war Labour government was seriously flawed; perhaps, in relation to the long-term future of its reforms, fatally flawed.

CONCLUSION

British socialists did soon begin to perceive at least some on the implications of such developments. By the late 1950s, and increasingly in the following decades, critiques of the British post-war model of socialism were articulated.

On the right of the movement there was growing unease about the insensitive and unresponsive administration of social services. Centralization in government was attacked with calls for devolution of power. Above all, corporatism, seen as the product of the old emphasis on public ownership and planning, was identified as the root of the problem.

Amongst some on the left rethinking was even more extensive, partly as a consequence of conscience-stricken revulsion from the Soviet system. There was a revived interest in democratic theory with great emphasis on the participatory model. Renewed calls for workers' control in industry and more widely for a 'democratic economy' could be heard.

But while there was much agreement about the general nature of the problem, there was less about its causes and almost none about the appropriate remedies. This was one reason why the rethinking bore remarkably little fruit in Labour Party policy or in the deeds of socialists where they had the power to act. The image of British socialism remained largely as it had been formed in that period of maximum socialist influence on British life in the 1940s. The road lay open for the political Right to portray socialism as intrinsically inimical to democracy and to suggest that only in abandoning socialist purpose could popular power and control be achieved.

NOTES

1. Doreen Massey, Lynne Segal and Hilary Wainwright, 'And Now for the Good News', in James Curran (ed.), *The Future of the Left* (Polity Press, 1984) p. 215.
2. Colin Leys, 'The Rise of the Authoritarian State', in Curran, *The Future of the Left*, pp. 62–5.
3. Labour and the New Social Order (The Labour Party, 1918) p. 9.
4. Quoted in C. Tsuzuki, *Edward Carpenter* (Cambridge University Press, 1980) p. 45.
5. Edward Carpenter, *Towards Democracy* (George Allen and Unwin, 1921) p. 263.
6. Ibid., p. 62.
7. William Morris, lecture to the Hammersmith Branch of the Socialist

League, November 1887, reprinted in A. L. Morton, *Political Writings of William Morris* (Lawrence and Wishart, 1979) p. 188.
8. William Morris, *News from Nowhere*, edited by James Redford (Routledge and Kegan Paul, 1977) p. 63.
9. Ibid., p. 74.
10. Ibid., p. 75.
11. J. Ramsay MacDonald, *Socialism and Society* (Independent Labour Party, 1908) p. 47.
12. Ibid., p. 81.
13. Ibid., pp. 171–2.
14. For an account of these lectures see A. M. McBriar, *Fabian Socialism and English Politics, 1884–1918* (Cambridge University Press, 1962) pp. 75–7.
15. This term is used by C. B. Macpherson in *The Life and Times of Liberal Democracy* (Oxford University Press, 1977) to describe the model of democracy adopted by the early exponents of liberal democracy in Britain. Macpherson's account of the different models of democracy provides a background to the understanding of democracy in this chapter.
16. G. D. H. Cole, *Guild Socialism Re-stated* (Leonard Parsons, 1921) p. 31.
17. Ibid., p. 12.
18. Ibid., p. 13.
19. Ibid., pp. 158–9.
20. S. and B. Webb, *A Constitution for the Socialist Commonwealth of Great Britain* (S. and B. Webb for the Trade Unionists of the United Kingdom, 1920) pp. 145–6.
21. Ibid., p. 158.
22. R. H. Tawney, *Equality* (George Allen and Unwin, 1964) p. 193.
23. Ibid., p. 191.
24. Ibid., p. 202.
25. E. F. M. Durbin, *The Politics of Democratic Socialism* (The Labour Book Service, 1940) p. 255.
26. Ibid., p. 235.
27. Ibid., p. 236.
28. Ibid., p. 272.
29. Ibid., pp. 283–4.
30. Ibid., p. 315.
31. Aneurin Bevan, *In Place of Fear* (Quartet Books, 1978) pp. 25–6.
32. Ibid., p. 30.
33. Ibid., pp. 127–30.
34. C. A. R. Crosland, *The Future of Socialism* (Jonathan Cape, 1980) p. 57.
35. Ibid., pp. 254–5.

10 The New Conception of Democracy under Perestroika

Richard Sakwa

Together with perestroika and glasnost, democratization was one of the three major programmes at the heart of the party-guided reform process of perestroika launched by Gorbachev after 1985. From 1987 a debate over the nature and forms of the new type of democracy suitable for the Soviet Union gathered pace, a debate inextricably linked with a discussion about the aims and viability of socialism in the modern world. The philosophical revolution that accompanied perestroika was known as 'the new political thinking'; and this new thinking in many respects reversed traditional Soviet notions of democracy and socialism and the relationship between the two. By 1990 the leading role of the communist party began to give way to a multi-party system, and thus the dissolution of perestroika gave way to the reconstitution of conventional Western-type politics. We will restrict ourselves to the five years of perestroika, from 1985 to 1990, beginning with a brief look at some of the old Soviet ideas about democracy before 1985, an examination of the theoretical bases of the new democracy, a short discussion of how the new theories worked in practice, and then draw some tentative conclusions on the feasibility of the new conception of democracy.

THE TRADITIONAL SOVIET VIEW OF DEMOCRACY

In a book published in 1978, *Criticism of the Ideology of 'Democratic Socialism'*, V. A. Nikitin sought to demonstrate that the concept of 'democratic socialism' was an unoriginal and conformist ideology based on utopianism and a futurological view of the world, and argued that it was an anticommunist and a pseudo-anticapitalist notion, barely distinguishable from bourgeois-liberalism and permeated with Christian social teachings. It was, he argued, nothing less than revisionism and indeed linked to neo-fascism.[1] This uncompromising stand was intended not only as a forthright attack on the Eurocommunism espoused by the Italian and Spanish communist parties, but also as an oblique attack on Soviet political scientists themselves, notably G. Shakhnazarov, who pointed out that the very nature of the modern world had changed and that the Soviet Union ignored this at its own peril.[2]

The old Soviet view insisted that democracy is limited by the socio-economic level of society, and thus established a fateful dependency between the level of economic development and civic rights.[3] This dependency was further buttressed by the insistence that political rights were subordinate to social and economic rights. The latter were 'over-determined' in the sense that they became, however patchy their achievement in practice may have been, the focus of the whole Soviet project of developmental socialism and the source of whatever legitimacy the welfarist neo-Stalinist politics of the post-Stalin years may have had. The evolution of the Soviet system from 1918 to 1985 can be seen as taking place within the framework of an economistic definition of socialism, whose main criteria were the abolition of the private ownership of the means of production and the collective management of the economy in the framework of the class power of the working class and universal planning. This economistic, or productivist, definition of socialism stressed the relationship between *things*, expressed in terms of ownership, rather than the quality of the relationships between *people*. The counterpart of the planned economy was a guided, or *dirigiste*, democracy in which politics, like the economy, was not to be left to the anarchic and uncontrolled forces of the market or the forum.

The traditional socialist ideal of self-management, a producers' democracy, was subordinated to rigid centralization and the productivist stress on one-person management. Moreover, while egalitarianism was condemned by Stalin in 1931, during neo-Stalinism from 1953 it became a cardinal feature of the neo-Stalinist compact. This contract, which of course was implicit and not codified in any specific way, operated in its starkest and most effective form in Czechoslovakia from 1968 to 1989. In return for the state's commitment to improved standards of living and welfare, the population was not to make excessive demands on the political system.[4] The new Soviet ideas on democracy emerged not out of Stalinism full-blown, but out of the stifling pettiness of Brezhnevite neo-Stalinism. The new democracy was a reaction to the apparent block on the evolution of the Soviet political system since at least the 1970s, mired as it was in the paternalistic notion of 'developed socialism' in the states of 'really existing socialism'. The new ideas, moreover, sought to understand the limited political development of the whole post-Stalin era.

Soviet conceptions of democracy have evolved and have gone through several stages, beginning with the notion of the dictatorship of the proletariat to the idea introduced in 1961 of the state of the whole people. The question arises whether the new conception of democracy under perestroika represented only the continued evolution of Soviet thinking, whose roots can be found in earlier notions, or whether indeed the new ideas marked an 'epistemological break', a genuinely 'new democracy'. In the following discussion the elements of novelty have been highlighted, though it should be stressed that the Soviet democratic revolution was not yet over, and much of the old remained.

THEORETICAL BASES OF THE NEW CONCEPTION OF DEMOCRACY

By 1987 Andropov's authoritarian perestroika was transformed into Gorbachev's democratic perestroika. The debate over the new concept of democracy sought not only to come to terms with Stalinism and totalitarianism but also strove to understand the roots of Brezhnevite stagnation. An essential feature of the new conception was a critique of the earlier Soviet theory and practice of democracy. It was now admitted that for decades 'democratic principles in our country were weakened', and failed to correspond to the 'political maturity of the masses'. 'The lack of development of democracy is the main reason for such negative phenomena as the alienation of citizens from the institutions of power and social apathy, which are only now being overcome.' From this it followed that the overriding task of perestroika was 'to develop the democracy and humanitarianism of socialism'.[5] The basic question exercising the reform communists was why Stalin could so easily create what the economist Gavriil Popov dubbed the 'administrative command system', and why it was so difficult for democratic perestroika to overcome Stalin's legacy. The debate over Stalin's destruction of Soviet democracy was the starting point for the re-evaluation of democracy, but it soon went on to examine the remarkable pertinacity of the Stalinist system through two generations of Soviet leaders and the source and consequences of what could be called the 'democratic deficit' in the politics of Lenin and the philosophy of Marx.

The new Soviet conception of democracy, and indeed the east European revolutions of 1989–90, were part of what can be called the 'second democratic revolution', if the first is the process that began with the English revolution and culminated in what Palmer called the democratic revolution of the eighteenth century in America and France.[6] Indeed, the debate over democracy during perestroika represented a continuation of the dialectic between the 'bourgeois democratic' ideals represented by the French revolution of 1789 and the socialist challenge of the nineteenth and early twentieth centuries, and at the same time renewed the struggle between the February 1917 'bourgeois democratic' revolution, which was only a belated extension of the French revolution to Russia, and the Bolshevik revolution of October 1917. This second democratic revolution, like the first in 1789 and 1917, has three aspects. The first is the philosophical basis for the new democracy, the second is the socio-economic basis for democracy, and the third is the practical politics of democracy and the state.

Philosophy: the theoretical basis for the new democracy

Gorbachev, Vadim Medvedev and Aleksandr Yakovlev all contributed to the development of democratic perestroika, but none could be regarded as the John Locke or John Stuart Mill of the socialist democratic revolution. These were all practical politicians, and there was little attempt to provide a grand synthesis of a new type of socialist democracy. Such a synthesis would have to come to terms with the plunge into authoritarianism of all revolutionary socialist states and would have to propose a new theory to transcend the historical legacy and generate a new type of democracy of socialism which was more than liberal democracy clothed in socialist rhetoric. While no such synthesis emerged, and perhaps could not emerge, there were, nevertheless, plenty of contributions towards a theory of the 'new democracy'. Analysis of Stalinism and how to overcome it provided a framework for the move from history to political theory.

Democratic perestroika focused on the 'indivisibility (*slitnost'*) of socialism with democracy and humanism', and took up the young Marx's aphorism that 'In a democracy people don't exist for the law, but the law exists for people'. The new emphasis on humanitarianism emphasized four aspects: the individual as the heart of the socialist project; mass participation in the state; a new approach to law; and an understanding of the spiritual needs of the people.[7] In other words, most of what had once distinguished socialism from liberalism, such as the attempt to overcome alienating property relations, class exploitation or inequality, was reconceptualized and thus the way became clear for a historic reconciliation of revolutionary socialism with social democracy.

The source of the new humanism in Soviet thinking was above all associated with the ideas attributed to 'the young Marx'. Allegedly there was an 'epistemological break' between a younger, more humanist Marx, concerned above all with human alienation; and a solid old Marx concerned with the dismal science of economics, surplus value, commodity fetishism and so on, to the detriment of the aspirations of the younger Marx.[8] The new thinking indeed stresses the elements associated with the young Marx, whether such a person existed or not. Marx's thinking on Russia for example, contrary to the partisans of the two Marx's, shows an extraordinary degree of continuity. In his last years he saw the onset of socialism in Russia as an imminent possibility, a socialism which could use the peasant commune as its base. In other words, a non-economistic Marx emerged who attacked some of the more dogmatic Russians as 'more Marxist than Marx'. This humanistic 'old Marx' could envisage a socialism based not on the development of capitalism but on its avoidance, that is, on human relations, and thus came remarkably close to the views of the Populists in sharp contrast to the Marxism of his more dogmatic successors.[9]

However, while a more humanistic Marx began to emerge in the thinking of the new Soviet democrats, he was also being turned on his head. The re-evaluation of the Soviet past and the new honesty in examining the history of the Russian revolution entailed a re-evaluation of Marx and Marxism as well. In this respect we see the old Hegel taking his revenge on the young Marx: the cunning of history turned against the latter. The Young Hegelians, Marx included, had accepted the form in which Hegel posed questions but had rejected his solutions. In his *Philosophy of Right* Hegel had argued that the individualism and atomization of civil society led to the strife of selfish interests. This could only be overcome through the mechanism of the state which established the true community of interest which was absent in civil society. Only the state could achieve the reconciliation of particular and general interests. Marx accepted the distinction between the general and the particular but, like all Young Hegelians, could not envisage the Prussian state, with which they were more often than not in conflict, as the reconciliator of the two. Marx went further and ultimately rejected the view that any state, and not only the Prussian one, could reconcile the general (the universal) and the particular (the individual), or overcome the atomization of civil society. For Marx the universalization of capitalism would eliminate the vestiges of particularity and when things had been simplified to the basic clash between the proletariat and the bourgeoisie, the former, the 'universal class', would overthrow the latter and with it the existing relations of production, class divisions and particularity.

The new thinking on democracy now hailed (with certain provisos) the differentiation of society and the particularism of civil society: the individual, that is, the particular, is the measure of all, according to the new Soviet humanism.[10] The new thinking represented the partial triumph of particularism and the rejection of the universal, in whatever form, the state or class. This should be qualified, however, to the degree that the new conception of Soviet democracy, a type of commune democracy, still assumed until 1989 a basic unity of interest in society, expressed in the leading role of the party, and thus the egotistical passions and conflicts typical of civil society were still a long way from being fully legitimated.

A dynamic tension emerged between two contrasting principles of social organization: the particularizing tendencies of civil society, and the universalizing aspirations of commune democracy. These two trends lay at the basis of the debate over democracy in the USSR during perestroika.

While the universal began to give way to the particular, Marx's attempt to achieve some sort of human solidarity and a community of interest, albeit no longer on a world scale, remained at the heart of Soviet notions of democracy. As the editors of *Kommunist* put it, the major task of the communist party was 'To preserve and confirm [its] vanguard role in conditions of democratic pluralism, not claiming a monopoly on political power but not allowing organisational and ideological amorphousness.'[11] We will return to the notion of commune democracy, but in the meantime we should note yet one more implicit critique of Marx in the new democracy, this time directed against his method. For Marx human community was both aim and method, whereas for Hegel his logic and categories enjoyed an independent existence. Marx accepted Feuerbach's argument that humanity was basic and that there could be no method or logic outside humanity, the corollary of which was that human society takes primacy over the human individual. The de-ideologization of Soviet thinking as part of the new conception of democracy no longer accepted this approach to human thought, that is, ideology, and suggested that certain categories have an existence outside of human society, certain human values are indeed universal. Not only Hegel's categories but also his method were vindicated. The new humanism thus opened the door to an acceptance of Kantian social ethics and normative philosophy.

One further point before moving on to more practical concerns. Not only did the new thinking vindicate Hegel contra Marx, but also A. A. Bogdanov was vindicated contra Lenin. This covered almost every aspect of Lenin's thinking on the party, its organization and role in society. Lenin's theory of the party emerged out of Georgii Plekhanov's determinist view of history which saw socialism as the inevitable outcome of economic development. If indeed there was a direction in history leading to socialism, then it was obvious that a committed socialist should use all means at his or her disposal to reach that point by the most effective means possible. As Posadovskii put it at the 2nd congress of the Russian Social Democratic Labour Party (RSDLP) in 1903, 'There is not a single one among the principles of democracy which we ought not to subordinate *to the interests of our party*.'[12] Bogdanov rejected such a fundamentally metaphysical view, further developed in Lenin's *Materialism and Empirocriticism* of 1909, which established an ontology of ultimate reality and absolute truth.[13]

And so do modern Soviet thinkers. There is now an end to what Karl Popper called historicism, the belief that the meaning and path of history are knowable. If history is not quite so discernable, then philosophy can be more open-ended, and a space opens up for more democratic and contestatory politics. This was yet another aspect of the de-ideologization of Soviet politics which the conservatives saw as the collapse of philosophical and ideological certainty. The return of Bogdanov's idea that the revolutionary movement should begin not from certain *a priori* principles but from the concrete needs of the workers and society is one which the new thinkers now shared. Bogdanov's implicit ideas on hegemony and an interactive relationship between the revolutionary party and the class can be seen as an early attempt to come to terms with questions that were later developed by Antonio Gramsci.

Economics: the socio-economic basis for the new democracy

The second aspect of the new thinking on democracy was an examination of the relationship between politics and economics, the socio-economic basis for democracy. The problem is the central one facing all those today who are in any way loyal to the Saint-Simon, Marx and Bellamy view of socialism as to some degree involving the centralization of production. Control over those entrusted with the management of the planned society was not envisaged as a problem, though it was assumed that it would be democratic.[14] In the Soviet context it was now recognized that the 'administrative command system' did in fact emerge out of nationalized property, and its bureaucracy was a class in all but name. A. S. Tsipko, the author of one of the most penetrating analyses of the ideological and political roots of Stalinism, considered that it emerged out of the Marxist revolutionary tradition. He condemned those who saw Stalinism as emerging out of the Russian patriarchal tradition and instead argued that 'Russian patriarchal conservatism had its faults. But it lacked the obsessive desire of our Marxist dogmatists to attempt once again to build life on the principles of a utopian Owenite commune, while shaking up the cultural legacy of human civilization in the process'.[15] The bureaucracy, however defined, together with the *nomenklatura* system of appointments, consolidated its power on the basis of universal alienation from power and property. The power of this class was now to be broken by a revolution in property and by the introduction of the market, described by V. A. Medvedev, the first chair of the Central Committee ideological commission from September 1988, as follows: 'The market, if speculative distortions are eliminated, is one of the greatest achievements of human civilization.'[16] Oleg Bogomolov added that 'Commodity-money relations, including healthy competition, are one of the most marvellous inventions of humanity.'[17]

The intellectual space for a new conception of democracy and socialism was achieved by the recognition that the laws of political economy were as valid under existing socialism as they were under capitalism. Socialism was not quite so planned, conscious or transparent as had been hoped. Moreover, the old view that the productive forces dominate the relations of production was modified by an understanding of the crucial role played by human relations, what became known in the jargon of perestroika as 'the human factor', in creating a dynamic and effective economy.[18] In this respect some of the ideas of post-Fordism have become an integral part of the new approach to the authority relations of the reformed Soviet democracy. The social relations of production are now seen to be a critical element in a dynamic and effective economy.

Moreover, the time scale and the difference between capitalism and socialism has been rethought. There is a new stress on the return to 'normal' life and culture, a 'normalcy' which looks remarkably like that prevalent in the West. The interdependence of the world, it is admitted, gives rise to a 'world civilised society'.[19]

While the democratic project of perestroika retained a belief in some sort of post-capitalist and post-liberal democratic fruition of democratic theory, as far as the economic basis was concerned a strong current of reformers in effect abandoned any sustained notion of difference. Moreover, as part of the reappraisal of the timeliness of the October revolution it was now admitted that the early revolutionary socialists were far too optimistic about the time-scale involved in the transition to socialism, a process that could be measured in decades and indeed centuries rather than years. As V. Vilchek put it:

> Capitalism gradually grafted on its differences from the feudal system and in the same way we will gradually reconstruct the characteristic patterns of life in a modern industrial society: market regulators of production, parliamentary democracy and a pluralistic cultural model. In short, we will converge, however compromised this term may sound . . . The fact is that we continue to think about socialism dogmatically, as a post-capitalist development, and not as a higher stage in the evolution of industrial society. We are extremely attracted by the successes of capitalism but are terrified by the word 'capitalism'. Why?[20]

The argument was taken further to insist that all the aspects of capitalism analysed, and implicitly condemned, by Marx were in fact essential elements of any industrial mode of production. By trying to eliminate them Soviet socialism destroyed not capitalism but the basis on which any industrial system has to operate. The market and commodity production were now seen as a variable independent of any particular social system. For seventy years the Soviet Union had struggled against the elements of rationality in the operation of an industrial system in the belief that thereby they were destroying capitalism. Vasilii Selyunin and Gavriil Popov suggested that any developed industrial form of socialism is by definition a form of state capitalism, reminiscent of Lenin's ideas of April to June 1918.[21] The alternative was Stalinism, 'industrial feudalism', or indeed some sort of synthesis of industrial and feudal socialism. In short, the new conception of democracy was accompanied by the emergence of a distinctive type of 'permanent evolution', where a revolutionary break and the ideas associated with it were seen as economically counter-productive.

The relationship between political democracy and economic life was the crucial issue and was much debated. Radical democrats insisted that without breaking the state monopoly on property there could be no effective political democracy. In a famous article Selyunin interpreted the history of Russia since the sixteenth century as the struggle between a nascent market economy and a repressive state. Economic progress in his account only took place when the market was allowed to develop free from the interference of the state.[22] The alternative to 'state capitalism', on which state socialism is based, was seen by Hungarian and Polish reformers, and a significant part of Soviet reformers, as capitalism itself. The more radical reformers in the Soviet Union, like Nikolai Shmelëv, indeed advocated the complete privatization of state economic assets. Others, like Popov, argued that the disbursement of some 50 per cent of the co-operatives and the private, individual sector would suffice.[23]

The argument returned to Friedrich von Hayek's classic treatment that political democracy requires economic pluralism. For socialists, however, as C. B. Macpherson put it in discussing Hobbes and Locke, 'Domination over things was domination over man.'[24] Tsipko, however, asked: 'Are sound guarantees of individual freedoms and democracy possible when all members of society work for the proletarian state for wages and have no independent sources of existence? The central question was whether 'a non-barracks-type, democratic socialism [could] be built on a noncommodity, nonmarket foundation'.[25]

Politics: building the democratic state

The politics of democracy inspired a re-evaluation of the role of the state in society and the principles underlying its organization. It should be stressed that discussion of the issue was conducted against the backcloth of a shift in discourse from notions of the 'state' to an expanding notion of a 'political system', allowing an evaluation of the various elements that can establish democracy accompanied by a growing lack of embarrassment about borrowing from the West. As Andranik Migranyan put it, 'What are the ideological and theoretical principles of democratic theory and institutional systems in the West, and what elements from this heritage are suitable for the revolutionary restructuring of our political system?'.[26]

The consensus in the early part of perestroika was that the Stalinist system emerged in sharp contrast to Lenin's understanding of socialist democracy as self-management. Under Stalin power passed to the party apparatus, and in the soviets from elected bodies to the executive apparatus.[27] The problem of *podmena* (substitutionalism) was strongly in evidence under Lenin, and his frequent denunciations of this remained no more than pious declarations. In the years of stagnation, despite proclamations about the need to raise the role of the soviets, state management functions remained firmly in the hands of party organs.[28] The basic motif of the new democracy of early perestroika was the attempt to spell out some sort of democratic Leninism, whose central feature was seen to be a self-managing socialism and the de-étatization of existing structures, from 'state capitalism' command socialism.

Traditional Soviet thinking, and indeed socialist thinking in general, on democracy has been dominated by two apparently contradictory types of discourse. The first is the statist, which has been analysed by Neil Harding, for example, in the notion of an 'organic labour state'.[29] This, at its mildest, was the sort of state paternalistic socialism so much criticized by the new right in the West and by the radical reformers in the Soviet Union. The second is what can be called the communalist, which stresses popular self-management and was developed by Lenin in his *State and Revolution* of August 1917, which was not much more than an expanded exegesis of Marx's views in *The Civil War in France*, with the notable addition that Lenin saw the soviets as the embodiment of a post-bourgeois political order. Both the statist and communalist trends were present in Lenin's own thinking, which allowed Lenin to be used as an apostle of the new democracy even though this meant suppressing the statist side of his thought.

The contemporary relevance of the commune model was declared on several occasions, and there was much debate over Marx's and Lenin's view of the Paris commune.[30] Marx, in his letter to N. K. Mikhailovskii, argued that the archaic Russian peasant commune embodied the 'principles inherent in his ideal' of an integrated human community.[31] One should stress, contrary to the partisans of the old

Marx, that for Marx economic development was always seen as a means to an end, namely to achieve human integration. Commune democracy is the political manifestation of this ideal. The discovery of this aspect of Marx for the Soviets meant ridding Marx of the 'accretions and deformations' of Engels and Plekhanov, to emphasize that the socialist project was ultimately a humanistic rather than an economic endeavour. It should further be stressed that this discussion of the commune model does not suggest a direct line from the revolutionary years to the present; such a mechanical view would distort the preoccupations of perestroika and the needs of a political system that once again tried to regenerate the idea, albeit with reservations.

The ambivalence over participation was revealed in the ambiguity of the role of the soviets. The soviets were meant to be at one and the same time organs of state power and bodies uniting the people in the nucleus of self-management and statelessness. For Lenin they represented a higher form of democracy than bourgeois democracy, which for him was always limited by 'capitalist exploitation' and thus always remained 'democracy for the minority, only for the owning classes, only for the rich'.[32] The political reform of the Soviet Union focused on the division of functions between legislative and executive bodies while preserving the authority of the soviets. The discussion of Lenin's view on this is extraordinarily confused, and ultimately held the civil war responsible for the legislative functions of the Central Executive Committee of the Soviets (VTsIK) falling into the hands of the government (Sovnarkom). All the evidence shows that this was proceeding at a fast pace even before the civil war, in early 1918, and that Lenin's attempts at legal and administrative reform after the war were half-hearted and at best ambiguous.

The genuine revival of the soviets was the key element of democratic perestroika, and this was to be achieved by the 'clear delineation of the functions of party and state bodies'.[33] The attempt to overcome not only the étatization of social life but also its partification could be achieved only by activating social organizations. The principles of commune democracy, embodied in the idea of the power of the soviets, was ultimately incompatible with a leading role for a party, let alone the earlier ideas of dictatorship of the proletariat.

The central feature of the commune model is the attempt to overcome the bureaucratization of modern political life. Marx's and Lenin's strictures against the state bureaucracy were now enriched by the experience of 70 years of a native Soviet *socialist* bureaucracy. Marx had outlined a series of measures against the bureaucracy, such as recall, the election of administrative posts, turnover of personnel, and for wages of party officials to equal those of a skilled worker. Lenin came to admit that bureaucracy had its own sources in Soviet life but ascribed it to the low level of culture in society.[34] In other words, rather than examining the political sources of the bureaucratization of Soviet socialism, Lenin preferred to focus on sociological factors.

The 19th party conference's resolution on bureaucracy insisted that it was the antithesis of democracy. In other words, the apparatus of the socialist state, previously lauded as the motor of social change, was itself now considered to have become a brake on the further development of democracy. The source of bureaucracy was now seen to be the administrative apparatus of socialism itself, which converted its own interests into those of the state.[35] It was now admitted that the administrative command system was a new historical type of bureaucracy, and that it was far more than simply red tape or a luxuriant officialdom. Soviet bureaucracy, in other words, was more than the sum of the parts of its bureaucratism but existed as a specific social phenomenon, whose roots lay not only in the sphere of power and administration but in the realm of economic relations, and in particular the formal nature of the socialization of property and the alienation of the mass of the people from acting as its master. Thus the notion of the 'bureaucracy' was given an almost Trotskyist centrality, though did not reify it to quite the same extent. The bureaucracy in the new thinking was to be combatted by, among other things, the introduction of different forms of property and commodity market relations. The bureaucracy thrived on the one-dimensionality of the old economy, and its monopoly was to be broken by the differentiation of the economy and the development of groups and their ability to achieve structured competition in the political sphere.

The fundamental problem of the new democracy was the classic one of finding an effective combination of freedom and democracy. The new democracy did not seek simply to borrow the proceduralism and formalism of liberal democracy but tried to generate a new type of 'humane, democratic socialism', as the Central Committee platform for the 28th party congress put it.[36] While the details remained vague, the basic emphasis was an attempt to combine the two elements of C. B. Macpherson's characterization of types of democracy: the protective democracy which tries to avoid the uncontrolled concentration of power; and the developmental democracy of John Stuart Mill which seeks to ensure the educative participation of individuals in political life.[37]

However, the second aim can come into conflict with the first, and by 1989 some of the commune aspirations began to be abandoned. Migranyan insisted that the Soviet Union was returning to the 'main highway of human history in the field of state building', to create a legal state.[38] The rejection of old traditions meant, according to Migranyan, that the USSR had created something akin to the Greek system of polis democracy where there were no guarantees for the rights of minorities and where 'dissidents' were suppressed. In effect, it was the dictatorship of the majority. Migranyan commented as follows:

> If in a polis this sort of democracy was possible, the attempt to create a single will in a country covering one-sixth of the world's land surface led to the total alienation of all from power and their subordination to depersonalised state institutions which themselves formulated the will of the people and represented it as it wished. Within the bounds of this 'will' the specific interests of the people could not appear. Now we have patiently to create democratic institutions, a mechanism of 'checks and balances', divide the functions of power, and introduce guarantees for the rights of the individual.[39]

The attempt to abolish the state through the application of commune democracy had indeed led to the end of the state as it is known in the west, but had given rise to the exact opposite of what had been expected, its 'endless strengthening and alienation from the people'.[40]

The point was that the destruction of civil society in the early years of Soviet power was a giant step backwards even in comparison with bourgeois countries. According to Migranyan: 'the state swallowed up both the individual and society', and in its turn 'party organs in effect swallowed up the state'. The totalitarian regime 'with its alienation of people from power and property was declared a higher form of democracy. This led in practice to the complete liquidation of a sphere of public power', and the destruction of the soviets as effective public bodies.[41]

While joining the main highway of state construction, Migranyan argued that 'in the field of political theory on questions of the organisation of power we are still on the level of Marx's understanding of the brief experience of the Paris commune, whose realisation in principle is impossible in a non-polis system and ignores our own rich experience. The history of the last seven decades shows that the implementation of this model of "direct democracy" in the form of soviets led to the complete alienation of people from power and to the dominance in society of an absolutely unlimited and unelected administrative management hierarchy'. Migranyan bewailed the fact that the institutional reforms did not achieve a separation between an effective executive and legislative branch. 'In the soviets we are once again creating a hierarchy of power in which executive power is subordinated to the legislative, and the legislative to a significant degree is subordinated to the party.'[42] In the absence of checks and balances, the separation of functions, or the participation of 'non-governing opposition parties', Migranyan insisted, the weakness of executive power at the heart of democratic perestroika could only be countered by the establishment of the 'firm hand'.[43]

The new conception of democracy associated with democratic perestroika was an attempt to find a new consensus combining the individual freedoms of liberal democracy with some of the traditions of socialist democracy. The new democracy sought to revive an autonomous tradition of democratic socialism. Its roots could be found in the tradition of commune democracy, briefly defined as the attempt to achieve a high level of mass participation and a degree of direct democracy which blurred the boundaries between state and society, and indeed which aspired to transcend the state altogether. This view of the new democracy did not pass unchallenged, and indeed was identified as the root cause for the plunge into authoritarianism. It was precisely the attempt to overcome the division between state and society, between political and civil society, that opened the door to the subjugation of society by the state. What was now called the utopianism of early communism prevented the constitutional definition of powers and thus provided no restrictions on arbitrary and ideological use of power.

The new democracy under perestroika tried to remedy this problem. It was a type of constitutional commune democracy, in which there was a constitutional separation of powers and the abandonment of the attempt to transcend the division between state and society. This allowed the crystallization of a genuine political society and, by the same token, encouraged the efflorescence of a civil society recognized (partially) by law and (to a degree) guaranteed by the state. The equivocations reflected the difficulties of overcoming the traditional practices and theory of Soviet democracy. Even a term for the new democracy was lacking, though the phrase 'socialist democracy' tended to be avoided because it was contaminated by the manipulative connotations of earlier years. Indeed, much of the lexicon of the socialist movement was tainted in the reformers' eyes and there began a vigorous process of cleansing the language of what had become wooden and theoretically meaningless terms. Moreover, the prefix 'socialist' to all and sundry was now dropped in favour of an adjectively unsullied and unqualified presentation of notions such as pluralism instead of socialist pluralism.

Constitutional commune democracy tried 'to combine the benefits of parliamentarianism with those of direct democracy', something which Gorbachev claimed to be a Leninist principle.[44] It was a hybrid form of democracy. Indeed, the new conception of democracy in its entirety was considered no more than the realization of the Leninist conception of (socialist) democracy, and this reflected more than the political necessities of the need to sell the reforms to the conservatives in the party. There is no reason to doubt that Gorbachev sought to find a new type of democratic Leninism based on self-managing socialism.

In so far as the new conception of democracy was a hybrid, it was contradictory. In particular, the stress on some of the proceduralism of liberal democracy was based on an acceptance of some of the ideological discourse of Western liberalism, but this was in tension with the alternative discourse of the Marxist critique of liberal democracy. This tension was reflected in the unstable practice of the new Soviet democracy that gave rise to the crisis of democratic perestroïka in 1989 and the emergence of the 'firm hand' of an executive presidency in 1990. The question remained whether it could provide the basis for the politics of feasible socialism.

THE NEW DEMOCRACY IN PRACTICE

There were some six key areas where the new conception of democracy during perestroika offered an original approach to the management of society.

The first was the new approach to legislative authority. Here Gorbachev urged the need 'to combine organically our Soviet tradition, born of the Socialist Revolution, with the universally recognised experience of the work of representative bodies in the world'.[45] In other words, the procedures of liberal democracy were somehow to be grafted on to the practices of a revived Soviet parliamentarianism.

The new structures created by the constitutional amendments of 1 December 1988 left a number of cardinal issues unresolved. In particular, what was to be the relationship between the Congress of People's Deputies and the permanently functioning Supreme Soviet, which was to be the main legislative body and at the same time an administrative body. Executive and legislative authority was in principle to be separated, and this was seen in the more assertive approach of the chambers of the Supreme Soviet (the Council of the Union and the Council of Nationalities), and the standing committees. From the first they adopted a vigorous approach to controlling the executive bodies, represented at the top by the Council of Ministers. The parliamentary scrutiny of the 57 ministers nominated by the prime minister, Nikolai Ryzhkov, in June–July 1989 saw several candidates rejected by the relevant standing committees, forcing the nomination of new ministers. The personnel of legislative and executive bodies were to remain distinct, though one result of the adoption of the American separation of power rather than a West European type of parliamentary system was the inability to question ministers on the floor of the legislative chamber. The standing committees also scrutinized all key appointments to state posts and ambassadorships, and took a critical approach to the state plans and state budgets submitted to them. The analogy with American Congressional oversight was no longer far-fetched, and the new institutions of a revived Soviet democracy were able in a remarkably short time to grasp the levers of powers by restraining the leadership, monitoring government policies, modifying legislation and in general reducing the traditional arbitrariness of government by ensuring compliance with the provisions of the constitution. The constitution, as in America, became the cornerstone of political practice. A new constitution began to be drafted to reflect the new political conditions, but the perceived transitional nature of democratic perestroika led commentators like Migranyan to urge a delay in its adoption.[46]

The second aspect of the new conception of democracy was a radical reappraisal of the rule of law in a socialist society. The new constitutionalism was based on the attempt to achieve a 'law governed state' (*pravovoe gosudarstvo*), proclaimed at the 19th party conference in June–July 1988. This spoke of the need to 'give legal defence to the individual, to strengthen the guarantees for the achievement of the political, economic and social rights and freedoms of Soviet citizens'.[47] The constitutional amendments of 1988 included the creation of a committee for constitutional compliance which was to act as a type of supreme court to ensure judicial control over administrative bodies.[48]

A legal state (*Rechtsstaat*) is not necessarily a democratic one, and this was to be achieved by the third practical aspect of the new democracy, the attempt to revive the participatory political mechanisms of Soviet society. An expanded notion of participation lay at the heart of democratic perestroika. The strategic course for socialist self-management was proposed by the 27th party congress, and was implemented in a variety of ways.

The status of Congress deputies was one of the key links between traditional commune democracy and the new parliamentarianism. All 2250 deputies to the Congress were equal, irrespective of whether they were elected to the 542-strong Supreme Soviet. Every year one-fifth of the Supreme Soviet was to be changed, giving a chance for others to join. Moreover, non Supreme Soviet deputies had the right to make up to half of the membership of its standing committees with the right to vote, and receive all information available to Supreme Soviet members. However, Supreme Soviet deputies were allowed a sabbatical from their workplaces and paid a special salary, whereas the others continued their normal professions. The aim was for these to be active in their localities, acting as a special type of link between the populace and parliament. The legacy of commune democracy remained enshrined in the right of recall of deputies at any time, a point condemned by Migranyan.[49]

The fourth aspect is allied to the point above: to achieve a degree of 'self-management' or 'self-administration' (*samoupravlenie*) in production. Even before perestroika various brigade forms of organization had been advanced by B. P. Kurashvili, of the Institute of State and Law, and supported by Zaslavskaya and Aganbegyan.[50] These were further developed by Andropov, and now under Gorbachev became a critical element in the practice of the new democracy. Kurashvili argued that the financial independence of enterprises should be extended in tandem with the democratization of industrial management.

The democratization of economic management took two forms, the election of enterprise managers, and the development of councils of labour collectives (STK). The Law on the State Enterprise of 1987 was a compromise, but self-management played a large role in it, with ultimate authority vested in the labour collectives which were supposed to establish a general strategy which was then to be implemented by plant management. This return to a notion of producers' democracy was very much in the tradition of nineteenth-century ideas of a socialist society. The election of enterprise management struck a blow against the administrative command system by depriving it of exclusive rights of personnel appointments through the *nomenklatura* system. The activation of the notion of a labour collective reduced the scope for administrative interference in economic life. However, the relationship between the state, enterprise management and the labour collective remained unclear.

The development of self-management in state enterprises can be labelled a form of political production democracy. It stood in contrast to economic market democracy, which can be seen in the co-operative movement and leasing; in other words the democracy which certain Soviet writers saw as emerging out of the operation of the market itself, with its pluralism, individual choices and so on, was contrasted with the democratization of the state-run socialist economy itself. The future of political production democracy remained uncertain and gradually lost ground to marketization and professionalization. Rather than embracing privatization or democratization, a middle path was sought in the form of long-term leases (*arenda*), renting out an enterprise in its entirety to the labour collective, and sub-units of the enterprise to those who worked there.

While marketization and democratization were to walk hand in hand, the cost appeared to be a loss in professionalization and economic efficiency. As L. Shevtsova argued, 'the needs of democracy and economic efficiency often fail to coincide, and even contradict each other'. Production democracy, she argued, has not yet worked in any country, and instead the world was pursuing business administration on the basis of one-person management.[51] Self-management was criticized on the grounds that the new soviets of labour collectives hindered the efficient transfer of labour and capital between industries, and thus impeded the emergence of a market economy. Self-management was seen as a way of avoiding the emergence of a market for labour as well as goods, and to prevent the dominance of a profit-led economic system.[52] At the second Congress in December 1989 Ryzhkov signalled a sharp turn against self-management and democratization in the workplace.[53] Just as commune democratic principles in politics were now being challenged, so self-management of the economy began to be denigrated.

The fifth aspect of the new democracy was glasnost and all its works. Glasnost focused on truthful information, including historical truth, together with a feedback mechanism. In other words, glasnost was not only a passive 'allowing all that is not forbidden', but an integral part of a new conception of a dynamic new democratic political *system*, and was often described in language reminiscent of structural functionalism. Glasnost was the essential basis for the 'socialist pluralism of opinions' but did not explicitly allow these opinions to be represented by organized groups, and certainly not parties until the onset of post-perestroika politics in 1990. Glasnost was therefore tainted by a certain instrumentality: however much its boundaries might be pushed back, the mere fact that there remained limits to permitted criticism meant that it represented the victory of the half truth over the out-and-out lie.[54]

The sixth element of the practice of the new democracy of perestroika was the democratization of the party itself. Here the new thinking had the furthest to go, but by 1989 rapidly made up for lost time. From September 1989, shocked by the stinging defeats in the elections of early 1989 to the new Congress and by the strength of the miners' strikes in the summer, Gorbachev launched a major debate over the democratization of the party in preparation for the 28th congress of the party, brought forward to July 1990. The party's role as the political vanguard of the people was to be strengthened during perestroika, but at the same time the party was to undergo its own perestroika. A new, allegedly genuinely Leninist, idea of democratic centralism was sought which could combine genuine activity by party members, openness and 'conscious discipline'. Gorbachev aspired to create a democratic party in a democratic society.

The party's leading role was gradually demystified and grounded in a severely practical need for guidance in a difficult transition to democracy. Gorbachev no longer justified the party's leading role in terms of charismatic legitimation and instead attempted to create a legal–rational basis for party authority.[55] The absence of a public sphere in the party clearly undermined the development of politics in society. However from 1989 the vigorous civil society that had developed in society began to invade the party and return it to the sphere of civil society in which parties properly belong. The communist party was 'normalized' and lost its Leninist mystique, and thus perestroika ended as a process of party-guided reform.

THE NEW DEMOCRACY IN PERSPECTIVE

Perestroika did not represent the end of the revolutionary tradition of October 1917 but its last stage, an attempt to democratize and humanize revolutionary socialism while avoiding the establishment of a meritocratic liberal democracy. The new conception of democracy represented a challenging approach to the idea of socialism and democracy, and there was much that the Western left could learn from Soviet debates. In particular, the attempt to achieve some sort of commune democracy based on production democracy, expanded political participation, glasnost and more open party leadership made the democratic experimentation of perestroika a unique phenomenon. In both politics and industrial relations the society began to move towards what Alan Fox called a high trust society.[56]

Few political systems can withstand the scrutiny of examining practice in the light of theory, but nonetheless this must be attempted. There remained several contradictions and problems in the new Soviet conception of democracy and socialism.

One of the major questions was whether the hybrid democracy of democratic perestroika was capable of providing a strong enough authority for the solution of the multitude of problems facing the country. Confusion over the exact nature of the new democracy led to a specific form of executive confusion: lines of responsibility remained unclear, above all between the party and the revived institutions of the state. Democratic perestroika was challenged from all directions, but one of the most potent was posed by the advocates of the 'new authoritarianism' like Migranyan. But as Leonid Baktin argued, 'why shouldn't a democratic power be strong? . . . Now in the USSR the population is learning in months that which normally would take decades'; and further 'Democracy does not provide ham and soap. But democracy gives greater hope that they will one day be provided'.[57]

The glaring gap in executive authority in 1989 emerged out of the dismantling of some of the excesses of the old *dirigiste* one-party state, and the lack of courage, ideological reticence and political stalemate which inhibited the full-scale development of democratic popular legitimation of authority, a popularly elected president or a multiparty system. Into this gap in March 1990 stepped the executive presidency.

Another issue was the compatibility of the concept of commune democracy with the attempt to achieve the liberal separation of powers and the rights of individuals. Just how effective was constitutional commune democracy as a basis to achieve a democratized form of Soviet socialism? After all, it was the aspiration to some form of direct and participatory democracy which had been used in the first place to justify the destruction of the proceduralism of liberal democracy. In its place not only had 'formal-display democracy' emerged, but also a type of 'public meeting democracy' which had left the levers of power firmly in the hands of a select group.[58] Having advocated a form of communal democracy in 1917, and having used it to justify the termination of the experiment with liberal democratic proceduralism begun by the February revolution, Lenin in mid-1918 turned against self-management in politics and economics.[59] This was not such a departure from earlier ideas, since *State and Revolution* itself contained not only a defence of the commune idea of politics, which attacked the allegedly specious liberal democratic separation of executive, legislative and judicial authority, but also sustained an argument in favour of an ill-defined notion of the dictatorship of the proletariat.

The dictatorship of the proletariat was now abandoned, suggesting indeed that the communalist tradition could now come into its own. However, there was a fly in the ointment. In place of the dictatorship of the proletariat the 'bourgeois state', and with it the egotistical divisions of civil society, returned, against which communalist arguments had been directed in the first place by Marx and Lenin. At first the Gorbachevite reformers did not consider this a problem since Lenin himself in his polemic with Bernstein had qualified his defence of the possibilities of 'primitive democracy' (that is, direct democracy), and had drawn on both Kautsky and the Webbs to argue that the 'primitive democracy', necessary in the transition from capitalism to socialism, should not be conflated with democracy itself. Representative institutions and full time officials would be necessary, as would specialists and expertise. However by the fifth year of perestroika it was clear that a choice had to be made between allegiance to commune democracy, however democratized, and the flowering of civil society. The new conception of democracy could find no way to integrate the thousands of informal political and social groups (*neformaly*) into the operation of the political system, a gulf that gave rise to a dangerous situation reminiscent of the dual power of 1917 and on which all sorts of dangerous forces could feed. The crisis of democratic perestroika had by early 1990 become critical.

The fundamental problem of any theory of commune or revolutionary socialist democracy is that it assumes a degree of political, if not social, homogeneity and a fundamental consensus on the structure and purposes of power. It contains a powerful totalizing, if not outright totalitarian, impulse.[60] It therefore inhibits the development of civil society without which there can be no effective state.[61] While commune democracy might achieve the accountability of public officials to popular forces by abolishing the division between executive and legislative functions, by recall, and so on, it failed to find a way of mediating between different interests. In other words, how was policy to be made, rather than simply ensuring its democratic implementation? The Rousseauist roots of the modern communalist tradition would suggest the presence of a 'general will', which in Leninist terms became the will of the working class, but all this is clearly unsatisfactory. Who is to determine the general will or the interests of the working class? For Lenin, of course, the answer was the communist party, and for Gorbachev – himself? The commune model, however modified by democratic perestroika, was still not an effective 'political form of the emancipated society', as Marx put it in the *Civil War In France*. No third way between dictatorship and procedural democracy has yet been found within the revolutionary socialist tradition.

As noted, the new thinking stripped Marxist democracy of its philosophical basis in denying the exalted view of the 'universal mission' of the working class. This allowed the rehabilitation of the state. Democracy itself was separated from class politics, allowing scope for a whole new dynamic of interplay between social forces and ideas: in short, pluralism, although it was still not provided with institutional expression in the new state structures. Plekhanov's economic determinism and Lenin's class reductionism were rejected in favour of social pluralism; the dichotomy between bourgeois and proletariat was transcended in favour of a humanistic understanding of democracy. The universal interests of the state or a class were rejected. It was a long and blood-stained path, and the only thing that might have justified the past is for the Soviet Union to have reached a stage where a new model of democracy could be implemented. It is for this reason that the commune model, and with it the revival of the slogan 'all power to the soviets', acted as the starting point for the development of some form of participatory socialist democracy during perestroika. But it did not last long. From within perestroika the commune model was undermined by a new emphasis on professionalism and proceduralism, and perestroika as a whole began to give way to multiparty politics.

The attempt to implement some form of production democracy raised all sorts of problems. Self-management was ultimately designed to buttress common ownership, and was firmly in the line of nineteenth-century socialist notions of democracy, but whether this could be inserted into a viable economic system became increasingly doubtful. The story of Yugoslav self-managing socialism did not add any lustre to the experiment. Moreover, the denunciation of egalitarianism undermined the whole point of economic democracy and exposed it to the populist challenge of organized labour.

In addition, while commune democracy is associated with a drive for statelessness, this is accompanied by an emphasis on the state (or the community) as the guarantor of equal opportunities and the provider of universal welfare. Hence socialist ideas of the state under perestroika had a double, and incompatible, edge, and no way could be found of reconciling the two.

The fundamental problem of the new democracy was the question of the compatibility of political self-management and the rest of perestroika, particularly the restoration of some of the practices of liberal democratic proceduralism and the rehabilitation of the 'bourgeois' state. Participation and liberal democracy, of course, are not quite as exclusive as those such as Schumpeter would suggest, though in practice the participatory element is subordinated to the procedures of achieving a government. There was a new role for the Supreme Soviet as a genuine legislative body, yet some of the old confusion remained, as in the proud assertion that the Congress and the Supreme Soviet 'not only issue laws, but also directly take an active part in administration'.[62] Soviet socialism under perestroika was still transfixed by an idea of commune democracy, the fusion of executive and legislative functions, even though the personnel were to be separated (apart from the local party and soviet leaders). The tension between self-management and direct democracy, on the one hand, and parliamentary proceduralism on the other, was at the same time both a source of confusion and a potential area of great creativity as the new Soviet conception of democracy sought to push back the frontiers of democratic theory. However, by the fifth year of perestroika it was clear that the failure to shift rapidly to democratic forms of legitimation, quite apart from economic and nationality crises, undermined the attempt to achieve a new synthesis of socialism and democracy.

At root the problem was the relationship between the role of leadership and democracy. Just as in Lenin's *State and Revolution*, where there were two discourses, the communalist and the dictatorship of the proletariat (the statist), so under Gorbachev there were two discourses, the self-managing one and the continued emphasis on elements of guidance and *dirigisme*. This operated at several levels, beginning with Gorbachev's own role as head of state and ending with the continuing role of the party as the vanguard of society. In an ironic twist to the democratic aspirations of Soviet socialism during perestroika, the same session of the Congress in March 1990 that renounced the party's constitutional right to rule by modifying article 6 of the 1977 constitution, strengthened the executive presidency elected not by the people as a whole but by the Congress alone, admittedly only for four years in the first instance. The dangers of the accumulation of power in Gorbachev's hands were often pointed out, but seldom with such power as by Sakharov.[63] There remained at the heart of the new democracy an exaggerated stress on the need for leadership while at the same time allowing the development of a vacuum of effective power.

The new conception of socialism under perestroika went far beyond Lenin's rather distorted productivist view of it as something akin to capitalism without capitalists. In *State and Revolution* Lenin noted that 'A witty German Social Democrat of the seventies of the last century called the postal service an example of the socialist economic system. This is very true'. Elsewhere Lenin argued that 'Industry is indispensable: democracy is a category proper only to the political sphere'.[64] The new thinking on democracy rejected this view, but at the same time hoped to achieve both professionalization and democratization in the belief that form and content can be separated: that the power relations of a marketized economy could in some way be combined with a democratic political practice. Indeed, thinking went further and suggested that democratic politics could only be guaranteed within the context of a mixture of forms of ownership.

Commune democracy in conditions of perestroika can be seen to have been no more than a transitional phase from the old 'formal display' democracy to some sort of post-communist democratic system. The hope of the commune democrats that post-totalitarian democracy would not also be a type of post-socialist democracy, or indeed pre-socialist, in other words liberal democracy, appeared to have been dashed. The attempt to revive the commune democracy tradition could be interpreted, for those of a cynical turn of mind, as a desperate attempt to find a politics of feasible socialism, but by the same token it acted as an obstacle to the development of a multi-party system and indeed liberalism as an ideology. The hybrid notion of constitutional commune democracy hoped to take what was best in the socialist tradition of thinking about democracy and combine it with the efficacy of liberal democracy. The problem was that it ended up with the worst of both worlds.

NOTES

1. V. A. Nikitin, *Kritika ideologii 'demokraticheskogo sotsializma'* (Moscow: Vysshaya shkola, 1978).
2. G. Shakhnazarov, *The Destiny of the World: The Socialist Shape of Things to Come* (Moscow: Progress, 1978); see also his *Futurology Fiasco: A Critical Study of Non-Marxist Concepts of How Society Develops* (Moscow: Progress, 1982); F. Burlatsky, *The Modern State and Politics* (Moscow: Progress, 1978).
3. Compare E. Kuzmin, *Pravda*, 24 August 1987.
4. G. W. Breslauer, 'On the Adaptability of Welfare-State Authoritarianism', in E. P. Hoffmann and R. F. Laird (eds), *The Soviet Polity in the Modern Era* (New York: Aldine, 1984); for the changes in the social contract under perestroika, see Peter Hauslohner, 'Gorbachev's Social Contract', in Ferenc Feher and Andrew Arato (eds), *Gorbachev: The Debate* (Oxford: Polity Press, 1989) pp. 84–123.
5. Yu. Solodukhin, 'Demokraticheskii potentsial sotsializma', *Partiinaya zhizn'*, 1 (January 1989) p. 7.
6. R. R. Palmer, *The Age of the Democratic Revolution: A Political History of Europe and America* (Princeton, 1959).
7. Solodukhin, 'Demokraticheskii potentsial', p. 7.
8. For an illuminating discussion of the alleged epistemological break in Marx's thinking, see David McLellan, *Introduction to Marx's Grundrisse*, 2nd ed. (London: Macmillan, 1980) pp. 1 ff.
9. See Teodor Shanin (ed.), *Late Marx and the Russian Road* (London: Routledge and Kegan Paul, 1983).
10. A powerful hymn to the virtues of a vigorous civil society was provided by an editorial, 'K novomu obliku sotsializma', in *Kommunist*, 13 (September 1989) pp. 3–24.
11. Ibid., p. 18.
12. Cited in Adam Westoby, *The Evolution of Communism* (Oxford: Polity Press, 1989) p. 231.
13. See Zenovia A. Sochor, *Revolution and Culture: The Bogdanov–Lenin Controversy* (Ithaca and London: Cornell University Press, 1988).
14. For an analysis of the inherent authoritarianism of centralised planned economies, see Alex Nove, *The Economics of Feasible Socialism* (London: Unwin Hyman, 1983); see also R. W. Davies, 'Gorbachev's

Socialism in Historical Perspective', *New Left Review*, 179 (January–February 1990) pp. 5–27.
15. A. S. Tsipko, 'The Roots of Stalinism: 1. On Zones Closed to Thought', *Nauka i zhizn'*, 11 (November 1988) pp. 44–55; in *Current Digest of the Soviet Press*, XLI, 10 (5 April 1989) p. 4.
16. V. A. Medvedev, *Kommunist*, 17, 1988, p. 17.
17. Oleg Bogomolov, 'Menyayushchiisya oblik sotsializma', *Kommunist*, 11 (July 1989) p. 37.
18. For the first major enunciation of this theme, see Tatyana Zaslavskaya, 'The Novosibirsk Report', introduced by Philip Hanson, *Survey*, 28, 1 (Spring 1984) pp. 83–108.
19. 'K novomu obliku sotsializma', *op. cit.*, p. 3; see also, among many examples, D. Furman, 'Nash put' k normal'noi kul'ture', in *Inogo ne dano*, edited by Yuri Afanas'ev (Moscow: Progress, 1988) pp. 569–80.
20. Vsyatoslav Vilchek's review of Yuri Afanas'ev (ed.), *Inogo ne Dano* (Moscow: Progress, 1988) in *Novyi mir*, 2/1989, pp. 265–6. For an English translation of this fascinating review, see *Détente*, 15 (July 1989) pp. 32–4.
21. V. Selyunin, 'The Revenge of the Bureaucracy' (pp. 192–209) and G. Popov, 'Restructuring the Management of the Economy' (pp. 621–33) in Afanas'ev (ed.), *Inogo ne dano*; and see Vilchek's review in *Novyi mir*, 2/1989, pp. 265–8.
22. V. Selyunin, 'Istoki', *Novyi mir*, 5/1988, pp. 162–89.
23. *Pravda*, 11 June 1989.
24. C. B. Macpherson, *Democratic Theory: Essays in Retrieval* (Oxford: Clarendon Press, 1973) p. 199.
25. Tsipko, 'The Roots of Stalinism', p. 4.
26. A. Migranyan, 'Demokratiya v teorii i istoricheskoi praktike', *Kommunist*, 1 (January 1990) p. 33.
27. Solodukhin, 'Demokraticheskii potential', p. 10.
28. Ibid.
29. Neil Harding, 'Socialism, Society and the Organic Labour State', in Neil Harding (ed.), *The State in Socialist Society* (London: Macmillan, 1984) pp. 1–50.
30. See, for example Solodukhin, 'Demokraticheskii potential', p. 8; L. N. Lebedinskaya, *O knige V. I. Lenina 'Gosudarstvo i revolyutsiya'* (Moscow: Politicheskaya literatura, 1988); and for the relevance of the commune model of democracy in the early part of perestroika see Richard Sakwa, 'Commune Democracy and Gorbachev's Reforms', *Political Studies*, XXXVII, 2 (June 1989) pp. 224–43.
31. See Shanin (ed.), *Late Marx and the Russian Road*.
32. Lenin in *State and Revolution*, cited in Solodukhin, 'Demokraticheskii potential', p. 8.
33. *XIX vsesoyuznaya konferentsiya kommunisticheskoi partii sovetskogo soyuza: stenograficheskii otchet*, vol. 2 (Moscow: Politicheskaya literatura, 1988) pp. 118–19.
34. Solodukhin, 'Demokraticheskii potential', p. 12.
35. *XIX konf.*, vol. 2, pp. 147–52.
36. *Pravda*, 13 February 1990.

37. C. B. Macpherson, *The Life and Times of Liberal Democracy* (Oxford: Clarendon Press, 1977).
38. Migranyan, 'Populizm', *Sovetskaya kultura*, 24 June 1989; see also his 'Dolgii put′ k evropeiskomu domu', *Novyi mir*, 7/1989, p. 175.
39. Migranyan, 'Populizm'.
40. Migranyan, 'Demokratiya', p. 34.
41. Migranyan, 'Dolgi put′', p. 174.
42. Ibid., p. 175.
43. Migranyan in *Literaturnaya gazeta*, 16 August 1989; 'Dolgi put′', p. 177.
44. Gorbachev's speech to the Congress of People's Deputies, 30 May 1989, *Soviet News*, 7 June 1989, p. 189.
45. Ibid., p. 188.
46. Migranyan, 'Demokratiya', p. 42.
47. *XIX konf.*, vol. 2, p. 173.
48. Detailed arrangements for the committee of constitutional review were adopted by the second Congress of People's Deputies in December 1989, *Pravda*, 26 December 1989.
49. Migranyan, 'Dolgi put′', p. 176.
50. Davies, 1990, pp. 15–18.
51. *Literaturnaya gazeta*, 19 April 1989.
52. A. Nekipelov, 'Iz plena mifov i dogm', *Kommunist*, 7, 1989, pp. 15–22.
53. *Pravda*, 14 December 1989.
54. A. Popkova, 'Gde pyshnee pirogi?', *Novyi mir*, 5/1987, p. 240.
55. *Pravda*, 26 November 1989.
56. Alan Fox, *Beyond Contract: Work, Power and Trust Relations* (London: Faber and Faber, 1974).
57. *Literaturnaya gazeta*, 20 September 1989, p. 10.
58. This point was made in criticism of commune democracy by Roy Medvedev, in *On Socialist Democracy* (London: Spokesman Books, 1975) pp. 140–1, and repeated almost verbatim by Migranyan, 'Demokratiya', p. 34.
59. V. I. Lenin, *The Immediate Tasks of Soviet Power*, various edns.
60. The classic case for this was put by J. L. Talmon, *The Origins of Totalitarian Democracy* (London: Secker and Warburg, 1952).
61. A point recognized by Migranyan (*Literaturnaya gazeta*, 16 August 1989) and many other radical reformers.
62. Solodukhin, 'Demokraticheskii potential', p. 11.
63. A. D. Sakharov, 'All Power to the Soviets' and 'Decree on Power', *XX Century and Peace*, 8 (1989) pp. 9–12.
64. Cited by Anthony D'Agostino, *Soviet Succession Struggles: Kremlinology and the Russian Question from Lenin to Gorbachev* (London: Allen and Unwin, 1988) p. 17.

11 Socialism and Democracy in China

Peter Ferdinand

TRADITIONAL CHINESE POLITICAL DOCTRINES

Contrary to what might be inferred from events in China in 1989, the principle of the responsibility of government to the people is in one sense much older in traditional Chinese political doctrines than it is in Western European political thought. Although government in China remained monarchical or imperial until the beginning of this century, although that traditional form of government and individual rulers were supposed to be sanctioned by divine forces, and although 'democracy' as a specific concept only penetrated China in the second half of the nineteenth century, it was nevertheless the case that the people had for centuries been seen in Confucian orthodoxy as the basis of the state – what has been called the *minben* theory of the state.[1]

What distinguished Chinese interpretations of divine rule from at least some Western versions was the notion that it was the responsibility of the ruler to achieve a harmony between the human and the divine worlds, and that if the ruler failed, then he lost the 'mandate of heaven'. If that were the case, then the people were entitled to overthrow him. Thus the doctrine of divine right to rule in China could support revolution.

In practical terms, however, this only amounted to a principle of *ex post facto* justification for rebellion. Although natural disasters such as earthquakes or famines could be presented as signs that a ruler was losing the mandate of heaven, it could only be proved that he had in fact lost it when he had been overthrown. There was nothing in the doctrine which urged rulers to go peacefully if they were confronted with public protests. They could and did use extreme force on occasion to put down rebellions. The Taiping rebellion in the middle of the nineteenth century – to take but one example – is estimated to have cost at least 20 million lives. Rulers could and did apply grotesque punishments and tortures to prisoners who had attempted to overthrow them.

As a state doctrine, Confucianism took an organic view of society. It envisaged a well-run state as being patterned after a well-run family. The head of the family had the wisdom and experience to decide all matters, and the various members of the family were expected to behave in predetermined ways towards the head of the family and each other. Thus every member of the family knew how he or she was supposed to behave in social intercourse. Provided everybody learnt by heart and properly performed their respective roles, the family, and the state at large, would be in harmony with itself, with the natural world and with the supernatural world. Great emphasis was placed upon ritual and etiquette. Knowing the rites was the key to harmony. Political relationships, like appropriate family relationships, were based upon texts which had to be learnt. The emperor was the ultimate source of wisdom, since he was the ultimate interpreter of the state religion of Confucianism. So in the traditional Confucian system, attitudes towards authority were bound up with the whole of culture. To be knowledgeable about what we would now call politics required a certain level of general culture – and we shall see that this attitude still bedevils discussions in China about whether the country is or is not 'ripe' for democracy.

Thus although rulers were enjoined by Confucian classics to keep the welfare of their subjects constantly in mind, there was nothing in Confucianism which allowed subjects to establish institutions which could monitor the actions of the emperor and which could check abuses by officials. There was a general preference for rule by men rather than rule by laws. Laws were regarded in principle as harsh and coercive, purely a means for rulers to oppress the people. It was better to rely for good government upon the benignity of rulers, who had been permeated by the humanism of Confucianist teachings, than upon legal guarantees.[2]

That is not to say of course that there were no checks upon the actions of rulers or their officials. In fact a feature of imperial rule from the Tang dynasty onwards (AD 628 on) was an institution of government called the Censorate, which supervised the activities of imperial officials and received complaints and petitions from the people about corruption. Nevertheless this remained an institution under the control of the emperor. There was no institutionalized check upon the emperor in the form of popular assembly right up to the collapse of the imperial system in 1911.

This notion of an abstract responsibility of the state towards the people combined with a lack of institutional mechanisms to operationalize the principle is a centuries-old feature of Chinese tradition, and we shall see that it survived right up to the twentieth century. Indeed it could be said that it is still a feature of Chinese politics today – although this is due to more factors than just the cultural legacy.

What it has meant is that natural human rights are not part of the Chinese tradition. Confucianism condemned any attitude which conflicted with the harmonious application of ritual or etiquette, and that obviously included selfishness and self-interest. There was no such thing as individual rights – and to demand them was the mark of the selfish 'small man', who was not entitled to any influence upon events. The only legitimate rights belonged to a group: family, lineage and community. And the head of any such group was bound by Confucian doctrine to display the same respectful attitude towards the emperor which he expected from other members of his group. So these collective rights were no bulwark against imperial power. Although members of the gentry in practice were able to exercise a great deal of authority over people living in their region, they were never in a position to demand the recognition of their rights *vis-à-vis* the emperor which feudal barons were able to impose upon kings in Europe. And even when the imperial system had broken down in the early twentieth century and there was a great deal of cultural iconoclasm among Chinese intellectuals, it was still very rare to find a consistent defender of self-interested individualism. It was accepted that it was the state which granted rights, and it was also for the state to determine their limits.[3]

THE PRC: 1949–76

The path to power of the Chinese Communist Party (CCP) in 1949 differed in various key respects from that of the Bolsheviks, but here a particularly salient one should be noted. The leading and mobilizing role of the CCP had been even more crucial than that of the Bolsheviks in Russia. Popular uprising had only been possible in areas where the Communists had been able credibly to provide protection against vengeful landlords, warlords or Kuomintang officials. There was no equivalent in China to the soviets as a symbol of spontaneous popular democracy separate from the party. The CCP had a monopoly upon 'revolutionary democracy'.

For the first thirty years of its existence the People's Republic of

China (PRC) claimed to be 'democratic', but it meant by this the same as the rest of the communist bloc. No institutions were created which allowed for serious regular consultations with the people or for serious responsibility of policy-makers to the people. It was the *People's* Republic of China in the sense that policies were supposedly formulated with the interests of the people in mind, and at the heights of Maoist enthusiasm it was claimed that the regime practised the 'mass line', that is, took ideas about policy from the masses and the brought them back to the masses in the form of concrete proposals which would faithfully embody those ideas. But even assuming the reality matched this theory, it still implicitly denied that the masses were capable of formulating mature and sophisticated policy proposals themselves. It also denied the masses effective participation in the actual formulation of policies in conjunction with the government.

There were many reasons for this lack of institutions. Some were cultural, some were historical, some were sociological, and some were theoretical. Apart from the legacy of cultural history already mentioned, as well as the self-interest of rulers in evading popular control where possible, perhaps four should be mentioned, just to emphasize the barriers which prevented any move towards a more genuine, institution-based democracy.

Firstly there was another historical legacy of China: the experience of China's near disintegration as a state in the first half of the twentieth century. All of China's new leaders were particularly conscious of her apparent social fragility, the sense that, as Sun Yat-sen had put it in the 1920s, China was 'a tray of loose sand'. They wanted to make the Chinese Communist Party the backbone of the new state, and they were afraid that if any serious institutional obstacles were put in the way, the result would be catastrophe for the nation. Even today that memory of China in the 1920s is vivid in the mind of a leader such as Deng Xiaoping.

Secondly there was the impact of Leninist ideology and the Soviet model of socialism. In the new China the image of the Soviet Union as the first socialist regime held sway until 1957, and the PRC consciously stepped in Soviet footsteps. So until that time the PRC leadership did not set itself the goal of developing a regime that was more democratic than the Soviet one. And when in 1957–8 China began its attempt to find its own road to socialism, democracy *per se* was not regarded as one of the top priorities. In 1957 Mao wrote in 'On the Correct Handling of Contradictions Among the People' that democracy was only a means rather than an end, because democracy is part of the superstructure of society and belongs to the realm of politics. In any case, throughout this period the regime was attempting to carry out radical social and economic transformation, and it felt that it could not afford wide latitude to real or potential class enemies.

Thirdly there was Mao's own personal distaste for institutions and a routinized way of life in general. As long as Mao was national leader, the life of the Chinese population was dominated by a series of mobilization campaigns, both big and small, to transform both nature and people's consciousness. In his eyes they seemed to keep alive the revolutionary spirit of Yanan. However ritualized they became, they made the new China *feel* different from the old one. And his fears about the possible disruptions which might be caused by too rigid institutions were exemplified by his treatment of his own party in the Cultural Revolution, when for several years it effectively ceased to exist, and when for the rest of his life it was a pale shadow of its former self.[4]

Fourthly there was the impact of the policies of urbanization, or rather non-urbanization. From 1957 onwards the PRC pursued a conscious policy of restricting the growth of the urban population, so that the proportion of the population who lived on the land in 1976 was the same as in 1957, that is, 80 per cent. The effect of this policy was to preserve traditional attitudes towards authority in the mass of the population.

The one distinctive Chinese attempt consciously to develop socialist democracy was at the local level. This was the establishment of communes as the basic cells of rural (and sometimes urban) life during the Great Leap Forward. They were inspired by the model of the Paris Commune and were intended to provide opportunities for ordinary citizens to make a greater contribution to the decisions which directly affected their lives. They were to be the basic cells of rural social organization, a nexus for decision-making about local production, farming, militia organization and social services. At the high-point of the Great Leap Forward they were even supposed to foster communal living, with the establishment of communal mess halls, and communal child-care arrangements. If they had indeed been genuinely democratic organizations, then they might indeed have represented an institution for popular control over all the facets of rural life. In fact, however, their average size was around 50000 people, which obviously restricted opportunities for direct participation in decision-making, and the leading cadres in the communes were treated as state officials.[5] Mao rejected suggestions to expand this model to the national level from Red Guards in Shanghai during the Cultural Revolution, which would have meant the establishment of a federation of communes throughout China. Then, in the early 1980s, the communes were abolished because, it was said, the very fact of the concentration of power at the commune centre had allowed unqualified local leaders to make incompetent decisions in too many areas of public life.

THE PRC SINCE 1976

Since Mao's death, however, the issue of democracy, or rather democratization, has re-emerged on several occasions, most graphically last spring. Why, given that it runs counter to all of the factors listed above?

Here three reasons can be noted. Firstly there was the common concern of many in the leadership and many in the population at large to escape from the arbitrariness and personal dictatorship which had characterized the later Mao years. As far as the party leaders were concerned, the guiding principle was to ensure that never again should any of them be subjected to the humiliating treatment of the Cultural Revolution. This did not of course necessarily mean that democratization (as it is usually understood in the West) was the answer. Rather what was needed to counter that danger was the re-institutionalization of political life – the establishment of genuine political institutions with their own rules and procedures which were stronger than any individual leader – and the introduction of a fuller legal system which would again restrict the freedom of manoeuvre of any political leader. For ordinary citizens too there was a pent-up sense of exasperation at the petty restrictions on daily life which had been imposed by the 'Maoists', coupled with resentment at the punishments which had been imposed upon individuals and their families in the post-Cultural Revolution years – it was later said by Hu Yaobang, when General Secretary of the party, that in the period 1966–76 one million Chinese had died for political reasons, 30 million had been persecuted, and 100 million had been 'affected', that is, they had suffered discrimination for one reason or another. Ordinary citizens, therefore, had a stronger wish to be able to exercise popular control over the actions of the regime, and that might mean political control. But equally it could also mean that there should be a stronger legal system, one capable of genuinely restraining political leaders.

The second reason for the emergence of 'democratization' as a political issue was that it came increasingly to be seen as both a prerequisite for, and consequence of, the economic reforms which the leadership after 1978 increasingly promoted. The move towards a more market-oriented economy, at whatever pace, was thought to require a corresponding loosening of direct political and administrative control in the economy. A market-oriented economy required the articulation of various interests to maximize the opportunities inherent in the greater flexibility of a market system.

The third reason follows on from this: in general the more highly developed economies in the world were also democracies. In so far as the goal of the leadership in the PRC was to promote a much higher standard of living for the people, and in so far as knowledge about the outside world become more widely available from 1978 onwards, then there was a natural and increasing predisposition to assume that greater prosperity and democratization in some way went hand in hand.

Thus the period 1978–9 saw the unexpected appearance of what came to be known as 'Democracy Wall' in Beijing. This was a long wall near the centre of Beijing on which increasing numbers stuck posters about matters of concern to them. These included poems, complaints about individual officials or housing conditions, memoires. But they also included demands from individuals for greater democracy in China. Though the specific forms which that democracy would take were not always spelled out in great detail, there were individuals who were prepared to demand an end to the party's monopoly of power, the possibility of a multi-party system, direct elections to the National People's Congress, and so on. For a while such demands were tolerated by the authorities. Indeed it was suspected that they were actually encouraged by the reformist wing of the party leadership under Deng Xiaoping as a way of discrediting their opponents, showing that those who were opposed to change were out of touch with the people.[6]

In 1979, however, once the reformists had consolidated their hold on power, the Democracy Wall movement was squeezed into silence, and a few of the leading activists were imprisoned for breaching state secrets. For people such as Deng Xiaoping the instrumental nature of support for democratization became quite apparent.

Yet within the apparatus other proposals for democratic political reforms continued to be formulated for another year or two. In October 1980 a senior policy adviser to the party leadership, Liao Gailong, presented a long report to a forum of the national party school in Beijing, at which he made various proposals for serious democratization of political life. He began by taking issue with Mao and arguing that democracy was an end as well as a means. People wanted freedom, that is, a high degree of democracy, as well as affluence. He called for a new constitution, the increased delegation of power to the elected regional people's congresses, the reduction in size of the membership of the National People's Congress and their division into two chambers, so as to allow deputies a more effective voice. One chamber would represent the interests of individual regions, whilst the other would represent the interests of various strata and enterprises nationwide. Although the details of this proposal were not presented, it seems as though it was envisaged that the second chamber would consist of members elected or selected at least in part on a kind of corporatist basis; in other words, there would be representatives of peasant associations, of trade unions, and so on. The two houses would jointly exercise the powers of initiative and legislation, and they would jointly supervise the work of the government. They would also check and restrain each other. For the time when the chambers were not in session (that is, most of the year) the Standing Committee of the NPC would need to be reduced in size from 300 members to a more manageable and effective 60–70. And the two chambers would also set up their own specialist committees.

In addition to these proposals for changing the composition of popularly-elected bodies, he also devoted a lot of time to the issues of democratization of the party's internal life, to the establishment of a more robust legal system and to the more effective separation of party and government institutions, and to the election within enterprises of representatives to congresses of employees which were intended to have a major impact (although exactly *how* major was left unclear) upon the business policy of the enterprise.[7]

These policies were as radical as anything which has been proposed by the leadership for the democratization of national political life. In fact most of them have never been implemented. Whether because of second thoughts, or because of compromises which the more radical reformers under Deng Xiaoping had to make with more conservative allies to preserve other features of the reform programme, or because of self-interest, the drive for radical political reform from the top gradually dissolved. Since then the regime has continued to talk basically the same kind of language of political reform that reformers in the Soviet Union and Eastern Europe were talking in the 1960s and 1970s. There was the need to make a clearer distinction between the roles of the party and state apparatuses, the need to free enterprise management from tight party control, the need to strengthen democracy within the party, the need for the party to do more to listen to the masses, the need to strengthen the legal system and provide a stronger legal basis for government actions, and so on. And, to be fair, changes have taken place. The legal system is now stronger and there are more lawyers to operate it than there were in 1976. Institutions have been established within the party to provide a regularized structure for decision-making, although that clearly does not prevent individual leaders from continuing to make a decisive impact upon policy in certain key areas and in crises. The state apparatus has been made more professional, and more work has been done to provide it with legal regulations to systematize its operation.

But in terms of actual 'democratization', as opposed to making the system more efficient, then the achievements have been relatively meagre. Leaders, even Deng Xiaoping, have called for greater democracy. In August 1986 a *People's Daily* editorial stated: 'It is far from sufficient just to allow the masses to discuss politics – we must actively encourage them to make their views on political issues known and provide opportunities and create conditions for them to do so'.[8] The National People's Congress does meet a little more often than before, and its deputies have become more critical of government actions, but it is still not directly elected. Deng laid down four cardinal principles at the beginning of the 1980s which were to guide all changes, and two of these were the maintenance of the dictatorship of the proletariat, and the leading role of the communist party. This was bound to restrict democratization. An article in *Political Science Research* in 1988 emphasized that any attempt to devise a theory of democracy in China today which sought to draw inspiration from a Rousseau-ist notion of popular sovereignty would be mistaken, since the government is still primarily responsible to the party rather than to the electors.[9] Direct elections of people's representatives have only taken place at the county level. And many of those elections have been competitive, although a restriction was imposed to the effect that overall there should not be more than one and a half to two times the candidates for the seats to be won. But Deng Xiaoping has said that direct elections at the national level would be unlikely before the hundredth anniversary of the founding of the PRC, that is 2049. And although the regime has specifically tried to win over the intelligentsia to its side in the 1980s by harking back to the slogan of 1957, thereby indicating that it needs positive inputs from the intelligentsia since the party does not know all the answers: 'Let a hundred flowers bloom, let a hundred schools contend', its appeal has been undermined by the fact that, as older members of the intelligentsia will remember, the original Hundred Flowers Campaign was immediately followed by a vicious anti-rightist campaign, which led to large numbers of intellectuals being stigmatized and even subjected to criminal sanctions for up to 20 years.

Now let us turn to popular conceptions of democracy in China today. As will have been clear from the above, one of the problems which has hindered the formation of a democratic consciousness in China has been the lack of a native democratic tradition. Indeed the very word 'democracy' is an importation from the West and is associated with the West. As much as describing a set of principles for the ordering of domestic political relationships, or a set of institutions to be found in some foreign countries, it has connoted an attitude towards the outside world, a readiness to accept that China has things to learn from 'advanced experience' elsewhere in the world. Thus it has been bound up with the more general debate which has re-emerged in China in the recent past as to how far China can rely upon its own cultural and scientific traditions to catch up advanced countries and how far it must import ideas and technology from outside. In turn this is an echo of the debate in China in the latter part of the nineteenth century over the relative importance of Chinese and foreign 'learning'. So debates over democracy in China cannot be divorced from broader cultural questions and from the issue of how far China could, or should, allow itself to become dependent upon the outside world.

For most people in China this is the starting-point, whether implicit or explicit. Popular attitudes towards democracy therefore tend to be divided to a significant extent by age. Enthusiasm for the outside world is most marked among young people, and so too is support for 'democracy'. A relatively small survey of opinion among students in a number of Beijing universities and colleges in 1986 showed that almost 80 per cent believed that the United States was the most democratic country in the world. The USSR came last, after the PRC. 96 per cent believed that China would need a long time to achieve democracy because of her long feudal cultural tradition. But this survey did not go very far in establishing what was understood by democracy. All it revealed was that 77 per cent disagreed with the idea that democracy meant the alternation of political parties in power.[10]

To gain a fuller idea of what at least some students may understand by democracy, let us turn to another survey which was carried out in Henan university in April 1989. Again this was a relatively small sample, so it is impossible to read it as a representative reflection of the views of Chinese students as a whole, let alone of the Chinese population as a whole. Nevertheless it is useful on two counts. Firstly the views are taken from the capital of a relatively poor and agricultural province, so that they may be more representative on a national basis than those of the 'gilded youth' of Beijing. And secondly, the views were collected just before the outburst of protests nationwide in spring 1989, so that they give a greater depth of insight into the sorts of things that students who were demanding 'democracy' in those protests actually had in mind.

Table 11.1 The most important feature of democracy (responses in %)

Rule by law and not by men	35
Honest government	20
The system of democratic centralism	10
Equal opportunities	7.5
Multi-party system	6.5
Division and balance of powers	6
Strong and powerful leader	6
Suitable standard of living	2
Fixed-term elections	1.5
System of multi-party cooperation	1.5
The majority principle	1.5
Respect for dissent	1
All-round government	1

Source: Zhang Tao, 'Daxuesheng dui minzhude renzhi, qinggan yu pingjia', *Zhengzhixue yanjiu*, 1989(4), p. 18.

What will be clear from this is the extent to which good, honest, law-based government is the overriding characteristic associated with the term democracy and not, for instance, the choice associated with a multi-party system. Indeed it is striking that democratic centralism was more often associated with democracy than the multi-party system. 65 per cent of respondents believed that democracy was the best system (though interestingly 19.5 per cent agreed with the proposition that if the Confucian principles of having a sacred ruler, and a ruler choosing to abdicate in favour of someone else, were applied again, this would be superior to Western systems of government), but as the compiler of the study notes, there is no clear expectation that democracy in China will develop along Western lines. Half of the respondents believed that democracy was either inappropriate, or only slightly appropriate, for China at present. And of that half 19 per cent believed that this was because Chinese cultural traditions were inappropriate, 24.5 per cent because China lacked a mature democratic environment, and 6.5 per cent because they feared that the ineffectiveness of democracy in China would lead to chaos and the breakdown of society.[11]

What these figures suggest is the extent to which democracy is still bound up in China with questions of culture (especially cultural 'maturity', whatever that might mean). Cultural traditions are still seen as extremely important, and the fact that China does not have a democratic one is regarded as a major obstacle to the development of democracy.

In turn this would suggest that popular pressure for increased democracy is weaker in China than in other communist regimes. It would suggest that citizens take more of a passive approach to the problem.

And yet it cannot be said that Chinese students in particular have been notably quiescent in China in recent years. Student demonstrations have led to the fall of two party General Secretaries. No one will easily forget the mass demonstrations which students in Beijing and other provincial cities organized in the spring of 1989. It is true that they were demanding 'democracy' amongst other things, but at the time it seemed as though they were primarily demanding the right to present petitions to rulers and to be heard, to demand the removal of corrupt officials. What they really wanted was 'good' or honest government. In this their actions resonated with Chinese traditions dating back to imperial times. And in general the leaders of student protests in the 1980s have seen themselves as trying to influence factions with the party leadership over policy orientation rather than demanding the establishment of political institutions which would entrench the permanent right of citizens to make their voices heard more effectively in political debates.[12]

At least, that is, until spring 1989. What became a key element in the demands of the students in May was that the government should recognize their Autonomous Students' Union as an official negotiating partner. Effectively they were demanding the right to restrict the power of the state to impose its will and they were nibbling at the leading role of the party. By doing so they were running counter to the centuries-old Chinese tradition mentioned earlier which conceded to the state the whole right to determine the nature of the population's rights. In the end this proved to be the sticking point as far as the party and government leadership was concerned. They would agree to meet with individual student leaders, but not officially recognize their Association – with the consequences which we know.

The effect of the subsequent government crackdown, however, will concentrate the minds of students, and others who supported them, on ways of trying to ensure that their other goals of a proper legal system and honest officials can be achieved and maintained. And in doing so, when contemplating specific new ideas to realize this, they will be thinking too about increasing democracy, whether or not that principle is specifically in their minds or not, and whether or not it is yet a proper part of the Chinese cultural environment. Ideas on institutions to achieve a Chinese-style democracy will emerge out of the concern to remedy specifically Chinese political and social ills, whether or not they have much in common with forms of democracy in other parts of the world.

The ability of Chinese to devise such institutions cannot be judged solely by the apparent lack of success hitherto. After all, the Confucian tradition, which was even stronger then, did not prevent the emergence of quite vigorous democratic institutions in certain provinces of China in the early part of the twentieth century, and these were institutions which could stand the test of comparison with similar institutions in other parts of the world at the time.[13] And the recent past has seen an upsurge of democratic activity on Taiwan where Confucian traditions are still stronger than on the mainland.

So although 'backward' Chinese cultural traditions may still discourage would-be democratic reformers in the country, the pressure to devise lasting solutions to the problems currently thrown up by her half-way house reforms, as well as to ensure that never again should anything like 4 June 1989 recur, will act as a catalyst for new thinking.

NOTES

1. Andrew J. Nathan, 'Sources of Chinese Rights Thinking', in R. Randle Edwards, Louis Henken and Andrew J. Nathan, *Human Rights in Contemporary China* (New York: Columbia UP, 1986) pp. 148–54; Andrew J. Nathan, *Chinese Democracy* (London: I. B. Tauris, 1986) ch. 5.
2. Zheng Jinggao, 'Zhongguo chuantong zhengzhi wenhuade tezhi', *Zhengzhixue yanjiu*, 1989(4), pp. 49–50.
3. Nathan, *Chinese Democracy*, p. 128.
4. Gordon Bennett, *Yundong: Mass Campaigns in Chinese Communist Leadership* (Berkeley: Center for Chinese Studies, Univ. of California, 1976).
5. For an account of life in a commune, see Anita Chan, Richard Madsen and Jonathan Unger, *Chen Village: the Recent History of a Peasant Community in Mao's China* (Berkeley: Univ. of California Press, 1984).
6. David S. G. Goodman, *Beijing Street Voices: the Poetry and Politics of China's Democracy Movement* (London: Marion Boyars, 1981); Nathan, *Chinese Democracy*, ch. 2.
7. 'A Report on the History of the Chinese Communist Party Delivered by Liao Kai-lung on October 25, 1980, at the National Party-School Forum', *Issues and Studies*, Dec. 1981, pp. 79–104.
8. Cited in FBIS Report FB 87-10003; compare *Deng Xiaoping wen xuan* (Beijing, 1983) pp. 134, 154.
9. Li Jingpeng, 'Shilun shehuizhuyi minzhude yunxing jizhi he lilun jichu', *Zhengzhixue yanjiu*, 1988(3) pp. 9–10.
10. Wang Fuchun, Wu Xiaojian, 'Guanyu beijing daxue xuesheng minzhu yishide diaocha baogao', *Zhengzhixue yanjiu*, 1989(1) pp. 24–34.
11. Zhang Tao, 'Dui xuesheng minzhude renzhi, qinggan yu pingjia', *Zhengzhixue yanjiu*, 1989(4), pp. 18–22.
12. Corinna-Barbara Francis, 'The Progress of Protest in China: the Spring of 1989', *Asian Survey*, vol. XXIX, no. 9, Sept. 1985, pp. 898–915.
13. John H. Fincher, *Chinese Democracy* (London: Croom Helm, 1981).

Index